The Python Language Reference

Release 3.6.4

Guido van Rossum
and the Python development team

February 03, 2018

Python Software Foundation
Email: docs@python.org

CONTENTS

This reference manual describes the syntax and "core semantics" of the language. It is terse, but attempts to be exact and complete. The semantics of non-essential built-in object types and of the built-in functions and modules are described in library-index. For an informal introduction to the language, see tutorial-index. For C or C++ programmers, two additional manuals exist: extending-index describes the high-level picture of how to write a Python extension module, and the c-api-index describes the interfaces available to C/C++ programmers in detail.

CONTENTS

INTRODUCTION

This reference manual describes the Python programming language. It is not intended as a tutorial.

While I am trying to be as precise as possible, I chose to use English rather than formal specifications for everything except syntax and lexical analysis. This should make the document more understandable to the average reader, but will leave room for ambiguities. Consequently, if you were coming from Mars and tried to re-implement Python from this document alone, you might have to guess things and in fact you would probably end up implementing quite a different language. On the other hand, if you are using Python and wonder what the precise rules about a particular area of the language are, you should definitely be able to find them here. If you would like to see a more formal definition of the language, maybe you could volunteer your time — or invent a cloning machine :-).

It is dangerous to add too many implementation details to a language reference document — the implementation may change, and other implementations of the same language may work differently. On the other hand, CPython is the one Python implementation in widespread use (although alternate implementations continue to gain support), and its particular quirks are sometimes worth being mentioned, especially where the implementation imposes additional limitations. Therefore, you'll find short "implementation notes" sprinkled throughout the text.

Every Python implementation comes with a number of built-in and standard modules. These are documented in library-index. A few built-in modules are mentioned when they interact in a significant way with the language definition.

1.1 Alternate Implementations

Though there is one Python implementation which is by far the most popular, there are some alternate implementations which are of particular interest to different audiences.

Known implementations include:

CPython This is the original and most-maintained implementation of Python, written in C. New language features generally appear here first.

Jython Python implemented in Java. This implementation can be used as a scripting language for Java applications, or can be used to create applications using the Java class libraries. It is also often used to create tests for Java libraries. More information can be found at the Jython website.

Python for .NET This implementation actually uses the CPython implementation, but is a managed .NET application and makes .NET libraries available. It was created by Brian Lloyd. For more information, see the Python for .NET home page.

IronPython An alternate Python for .NET. Unlike Python.NET, this is a complete Python implementation that generates IL, and compiles Python code directly to .NET assemblies. It was created by Jim Hugunin, the original creator of Jython. For more information, see the IronPython website.

PyPy An implementation of Python written completely in Python. It supports several advanced features not found in other implementations like stackless support and a Just in Time compiler. One of the goals of the project is to encourage experimentation with the language itself by making it easier to modify the interpreter (since it is written in Python). Additional information is available on the PyPy project's home page.

Each of these implementations varies in some way from the language as documented in this manual, or introduces specific information beyond what's covered in the standard Python documentation. Please refer to the implementation-specific documentation to determine what else you need to know about the specific implementation you're using.

1.2 Notation

The descriptions of lexical analysis and syntax use a modified BNF grammar notation. This uses the following style of definition:

```
name       ::=   lc_letter (lc_letter | "_")*
lc_letter  ::=   "a"..."z"
```

The first line says that a `name` is an `lc_letter` followed by a sequence of zero or more `lc_letter`s and underscores. An `lc_letter` in turn is any of the single characters 'a' through 'z'. (This rule is actually adhered to for the names defined in lexical and grammar rules in this document.)

Each rule begins with a name (which is the name defined by the rule) and `::=`. A vertical bar (|) is used to separate alternatives; it is the least binding operator in this notation. A star (*) means zero or more repetitions of the preceding item; likewise, a plus (+) means one or more repetitions, and a phrase enclosed in square brackets ([ ]) means zero or one occurrences (in other words, the enclosed phrase is optional). The * and + operators bind as tightly as possible; parentheses are used for grouping. Literal strings are enclosed in quotes. White space is only meaningful to separate tokens. Rules are normally contained on a single line; rules with many alternatives may be formatted alternatively with each line after the first beginning with a vertical bar.

In lexical definitions (as the example above), two more conventions are used: Two literal characters separated by three dots mean a choice of any single character in the given (inclusive) range of ASCII characters. A phrase between angular brackets (<...>) gives an informal description of the symbol defined; e.g., this could be used to describe the notion of 'control character' if needed.

Even though the notation used is almost the same, there is a big difference between the meaning of lexical and syntactic definitions: a lexical definition operates on the individual characters of the input source, while a syntax definition operates on the stream of tokens generated by the lexical analysis. All uses of BNF in the next chapter ("Lexical Analysis") are lexical definitions; uses in subsequent chapters are syntactic definitions.

LEXICAL ANALYSIS

A Python program is read by a *parser*. Input to the parser is a stream of *tokens*, generated by the *lexical analyzer*. This chapter describes how the lexical analyzer breaks a file into tokens.

Python reads program text as Unicode code points; the encoding of a source file can be given by an encoding declaration and defaults to UTF-8, see PEP 3120 for details. If the source file cannot be decoded, a `SyntaxError` is raised.

2.1 Line structure

A Python program is divided into a number of *logical lines*.

2.1.1 Logical lines

The end of a logical line is represented by the token NEWLINE. Statements cannot cross logical line boundaries except where NEWLINE is allowed by the syntax (e.g., between statements in compound statements). A logical line is constructed from one or more *physical lines* by following the explicit or implicit *line joining* rules.

2.1.2 Physical lines

A physical line is a sequence of characters terminated by an end-of-line sequence. In source files, any of the standard platform line termination sequences can be used - the Unix form using ASCII LF (linefeed), the Windows form using the ASCII sequence CR LF (return followed by linefeed), or the old Macintosh form using the ASCII CR (return) character. All of these forms can be used equally, regardless of platform.

When embedding Python, source code strings should be passed to Python APIs using the standard C conventions for newline characters (the `\n` character, representing ASCII LF, is the line terminator).

2.1.3 Comments

A comment starts with a hash character (`#`) that is not part of a string literal, and ends at the end of the physical line. A comment signifies the end of the logical line unless the implicit line joining rules are invoked. Comments are ignored by the syntax; they are not tokens.

2.1.4 Encoding declarations

If a comment in the first or second line of the Python script matches the regular expression `coding[=:]\s*([-\w.]+)`, this comment is processed as an encoding declaration; the first group of this expression names the encoding of the source code file. The encoding declaration must appear on a line of its own. If it is the second line, the first line must also be a comment-only line. The recommended forms of an encoding expression are

```
# -*- coding: <encoding-name> -*-
```

which is recognized also by GNU Emacs, and

```
# vim:fileencoding=<encoding-name>
```

which is recognized by Bram Moolenaar's VIM.

If no encoding declaration is found, the default encoding is UTF-8. In addition, if the first bytes of the file are the UTF-8 byte-order mark (`b'\xef\xbb\xbf'`), the declared file encoding is UTF-8 (this is supported, among others, by Microsoft's **notepad**).

If an encoding is declared, the encoding name must be recognized by Python. The encoding is used for all lexical analysis, including string literals, comments and identifiers.

2.1.5 Explicit line joining

Two or more physical lines may be joined into logical lines using backslash characters (\), as follows: when a physical line ends in a backslash that is not part of a string literal or comment, it is joined with the following forming a single logical line, deleting the backslash and the following end-of-line character. For example:

```
if 1900 < year < 2100 and 1 <= month <= 12 \
   and 1 <= day <= 31 and 0 <= hour < 24 \
   and 0 <= minute < 60 and 0 <= second < 60:   # Looks like a valid date
        return 1
```

A line ending in a backslash cannot carry a comment. A backslash does not continue a comment. A backslash does not continue a token except for string literals (i.e., tokens other than string literals cannot be split across physical lines using a backslash). A backslash is illegal elsewhere on a line outside a string literal.

2.1.6 Implicit line joining

Expressions in parentheses, square brackets or curly braces can be split over more than one physical line without using backslashes. For example:

```
month_names = ['Januari', 'Februari', 'Maart',      # These are the
               'April',   'Mei',      'Juni',        # Dutch names
               'Juli',    'Augustus', 'September',    # for the months
               'Oktober', 'November', 'December']     # of the year
```

Implicitly continued lines can carry comments. The indentation of the continuation lines is not important. Blank continuation lines are allowed. There is no NEWLINE token between implicit continuation lines. Implicitly continued lines can also occur within triple-quoted strings (see below); in that case they cannot carry comments.

2.1.7 Blank lines

A logical line that contains only spaces, tabs, formfeeds and possibly a comment, is ignored (i.e., no NEW-LINE token is generated). During interactive input of statements, handling of a blank line may differ depending on the implementation of the read-eval-print loop. In the standard interactive interpreter, an entirely blank logical line (i.e. one containing not even whitespace or a comment) terminates a multi-line statement.

2.1.8 Indentation

Leading whitespace (spaces and tabs) at the beginning of a logical line is used to compute the indentation level of the line, which in turn is used to determine the grouping of statements.

Tabs are replaced (from left to right) by one to eight spaces such that the total number of characters up to and including the replacement is a multiple of eight (this is intended to be the same rule as used by Unix). The total number of spaces preceding the first non-blank character then determines the line's indentation. Indentation cannot be split over multiple physical lines using backslashes; the whitespace up to the first backslash determines the indentation.

Indentation is rejected as inconsistent if a source file mixes tabs and spaces in a way that makes the meaning dependent on the worth of a tab in spaces; a **TabError** is raised in that case.

Cross-platform compatibility note: because of the nature of text editors on non-UNIX platforms, it is unwise to use a mixture of spaces and tabs for the indentation in a single source file. It should also be noted that different platforms may explicitly limit the maximum indentation level.

A formfeed character may be present at the start of the line; it will be ignored for the indentation calculations above. Formfeed characters occurring elsewhere in the leading whitespace have an undefined effect (for instance, they may reset the space count to zero).

The indentation levels of consecutive lines are used to generate INDENT and DEDENT tokens, using a stack, as follows.

Before the first line of the file is read, a single zero is pushed on the stack; this will never be popped off again. The numbers pushed on the stack will always be strictly increasing from bottom to top. At the beginning of each logical line, the line's indentation level is compared to the top of the stack. If it is equal, nothing happens. If it is larger, it is pushed on the stack, and one INDENT token is generated. If it is smaller, it *must* be one of the numbers occurring on the stack; all numbers on the stack that are larger are popped off, and for each number popped off a DEDENT token is generated. At the end of the file, a DEDENT token is generated for each number remaining on the stack that is larger than zero.

Here is an example of a correctly (though confusingly) indented piece of Python code:

```
def perm(l):
        # Compute the list of all permutations of l
    if len(l) <= 1:
                return [l]
    r = []
    for i in range(len(l)):
            s = l[:i] + l[i+1:]
            p = perm(s)
            for x in p:
             r.append(l[i:i+1] + x)
    return r
```

The following example shows various indentation errors:

```
 def perm(l):                      # error: first line indented
for i in range(len(l)):            # error: not indented
    s = l[:i] + l[i+1:]
        p = perm(l[:i] + l[i+1:])  # error: unexpected indent
        for x in p:
                r.append(l[i:i+1] + x)
            return r               # error: inconsistent dedent
```

(Actually, the first three errors are detected by the parser; only the last error is found by the lexical analyzer — the indentation of `return r` does not match a level popped off the stack.)

2.1.9 Whitespace between tokens

Except at the beginning of a logical line or in string literals, the whitespace characters space, tab and formfeed can be used interchangeably to separate tokens. Whitespace is needed between two tokens only if their concatenation could otherwise be interpreted as a different token (e.g., ab is one token, but a b is two tokens).

2.2 Other tokens

Besides NEWLINE, INDENT and DEDENT, the following categories of tokens exist: *identifiers*, *keywords*, *literals*, *operators*, and *delimiters*. Whitespace characters (other than line terminators, discussed earlier) are not tokens, but serve to delimit tokens. Where ambiguity exists, a token comprises the longest possible string that forms a legal token, when read from left to right.

2.3 Identifiers and keywords

Identifiers (also referred to as *names*) are described by the following lexical definitions.

The syntax of identifiers in Python is based on the Unicode standard annex UAX-31, with elaboration and changes as defined below; see also PEP 3131 for further details.

Within the ASCII range (U+0001..U+007F), the valid characters for identifiers are the same as in Python 2.x: the uppercase and lowercase letters A through Z, the underscore _ and, except for the first character, the digits 0 through 9.

Python 3.0 introduces additional characters from outside the ASCII range (see PEP 3131). For these characters, the classification uses the version of the Unicode Character Database as included in the `unicodedata` module.

Identifiers are unlimited in length. Case is significant.

```
identifier    ::=  xid_start xid_continue*
id_start      ::=  <all characters in general categories Lu, Ll, Lt, Lm, Lo, Nl, the underscore, and
id_continue   ::=  <all characters in id_start, plus characters in the categories Mn, Mc, Nd, Pc and
xid_start     ::=  <all characters in id_start whose NFKC normalization is in "id_start xid_continue*">
xid_continue  ::=  <all characters in id_continue whose NFKC normalization is in "id_continue*">
```

The Unicode category codes mentioned above stand for:

- *Lu* - uppercase letters
- *Ll* - lowercase letters
- *Lt* - titlecase letters
- *Lm* - modifier letters
- *Lo* - other letters
- *Nl* - letter numbers
- *Mn* - nonspacing marks

- *Mc* - spacing combining marks

- *Nd* - decimal numbers

- *Pc* - connector punctuations

- *Other_ID_Start* - explicit list of characters in PropList.txt to support backwards compatibility

- *Other_ID_Continue* - likewise

All identifiers are converted into the normal form NFKC while parsing; comparison of identifiers is based on NFKC.

A non-normative HTML file listing all valid identifier characters for Unicode 4.1 can be found at https://www.dcl.hpi.uni-potsdam.de/home/loewis/table-3131.html.

2.3.1 Keywords

The following identifiers are used as reserved words, or *keywords* of the language, and cannot be used as ordinary identifiers. They must be spelled exactly as written here:

```
False     class     finally   is        return
None      continue  for       lambda    try
True      def       from      nonlocal  while
and       del       global    not       with
as        elif      if        or        yield
assert    else      import    pass
break     except    in        raise
```

2.3.2 Reserved classes of identifiers

Certain classes of identifiers (besides keywords) have special meanings. These classes are identified by the patterns of leading and trailing underscore characters:

`_*` Not imported by `from module import *`. The special identifier `_` is used in the interactive interpreter to store the result of the last evaluation; it is stored in the `builtins` module. When not in interactive mode, `_` has no special meaning and is not defined. See section *The import statement.*

Note: The name `_` is often used in conjunction with internationalization; refer to the documentation for the `gettext` module for more information on this convention.

`__*__` System-defined names. These names are defined by the interpreter and its implementation (including the standard library). Current system names are discussed in the *Special method names* section and elsewhere. More will likely be defined in future versions of Python. *Any* use of `__*__` names, in any context, that does not follow explicitly documented use, is subject to breakage without warning.

`__*` Class-private names. Names in this category, when used within the context of a class definition, are re-written to use a mangled form to help avoid name clashes between "private" attributes of base and derived classes. See section *Identifiers (Names)*.

2.4 Literals

Literals are notations for constant values of some built-in types.

2.4.1 String and Bytes literals

String literals are described by the following lexical definitions:

```
stringliteral    ::=  [stringprefix](shortstring | longstring)
stringprefix     ::=  "r" | "u" | "R" | "U" | "f" | "F"
                      | "fr" | "Fr" | "fR" | "FR" | "rf" | "rF" | "Rf" | "RF"
shortstring      ::=  "'" shortstringitem* "'" | '"' shortstringitem* '"'
longstring       ::=  "'''" longstringitem* "'''" | '"""' longstringitem* '"""'
shortstringitem  ::=  shortstringchar | stringescapeseq
longstringitem   ::=  longstringchar | stringescapeseq
shortstringchar  ::=  <any source character except "\" or newline or the quote>
longstringchar   ::=  <any source character except "\">
stringescapeseq  ::=  "\" <any source character>
```

```
bytesliteral    ::=  bytesprefix(shortbytes | longbytes)
bytesprefix     ::=  "b" | "B" | "br" | "Br" | "bR" | "BR" | "rb" | "rB" | "Rb" | "RB"
shortbytes      ::=  "'" shortbytesitem* "'" | '"' shortbytesitem* '"'
longbytes       ::=  "'''" longbytesitem* "'''" | '"""' longbytesitem* '"""'
shortbytesitem  ::=  shortbyteschar | bytesescapeseq
longbytesitem   ::=  longbyteschar | bytesescapeseq
shortbyteschar  ::=  <any ASCII character except "\" or newline or the quote>
longbyteschar   ::=  <any ASCII character except "\">
bytesescapeseq  ::=  "\" <any ASCII character>
```

One syntactic restriction not indicated by these productions is that whitespace is not allowed between the *stringprefix* or *bytesprefix* and the rest of the literal. The source character set is defined by the encoding declaration; it is UTF-8 if no encoding declaration is given in the source file; see section *Encoding declarations*.

In plain English: Both types of literals can be enclosed in matching single quotes (') or double quotes ("). They can also be enclosed in matching groups of three single or double quotes (these are generally referred to as *triple-quoted strings*). The backslash (\) character is used to escape characters that otherwise have a special meaning, such as newline, backslash itself, or the quote character.

Bytes literals are always prefixed with 'b' or 'B'; they produce an instance of the `bytes` type instead of the `str` type. They may only contain ASCII characters; bytes with a numeric value of 128 or greater must be expressed with escapes.

Both string and bytes literals may optionally be prefixed with a letter 'r' or 'R'; such strings are called *raw strings* and treat backslashes as literal characters. As a result, in string literals, '\U' and '\u' escapes in raw strings are not treated specially. Given that Python 2.x's raw unicode literals behave differently than Python 3.x's the 'ur' syntax is not supported.

New in version 3.3: The 'rb' prefix of raw bytes literals has been added as a synonym of 'br'.

New in version 3.3: Support for the unicode legacy literal (u'value') was reintroduced to simplify the maintenance of dual Python 2.x and 3.x codebases. See PEP 414 for more information.

A string literal with 'f' or 'F' in its prefix is a *formatted string literal*; see *Formatted string literals*. The 'f' may be combined with 'r', but not with 'b' or 'u', therefore raw formatted strings are possible, but formatted bytes literals are not.

In triple-quoted literals, unescaped newlines and quotes are allowed (and are retained), except that three unescaped quotes in a row terminate the literal. (A "quote" is the character used to open the literal, i.e. either ' or ".)

Unless an 'r' or 'R' prefix is present, escape sequences in string and bytes literals are interpreted according to rules similar to those used by Standard C. The recognized escape sequences are:

Escape Sequence	Meaning	Notes
\newline	Backslash and newline ignored	
\\	Backslash (\)	
\'	Single quote (')	
\"	Double quote (")	
\a	ASCII Bell (BEL)	
\b	ASCII Backspace (BS)	
\f	ASCII Formfeed (FF)	
\n	ASCII Linefeed (LF)	
\r	ASCII Carriage Return (CR)	
\t	ASCII Horizontal Tab (TAB)	
\v	ASCII Vertical Tab (VT)	
\ooo	Character with octal value *ooo*	(1,3)
\xhh	Character with hex value *hh*	(2,3)

Escape sequences only recognized in string literals are:

Escape Sequence	Meaning	Notes
\N{name}	Character named *name* in the Unicode database	(4)
\uxxxx	Character with 16-bit hex value *xxxx*	(5)
\Uxxxxxxxx	Character with 32-bit hex value *xxxxxxxx*	(6)

Notes:

1. As in Standard C, up to three octal digits are accepted.

2. Unlike in Standard C, exactly two hex digits are required.

3. In a bytes literal, hexadecimal and octal escapes denote the byte with the given value. In a string literal, these escapes denote a Unicode character with the given value.

4. Changed in version 3.3: Support for name aliases[1] has been added.

5. Exactly four hex digits are required.

6. Any Unicode character can be encoded this way. Exactly eight hex digits are required.

Unlike Standard C, all unrecognized escape sequences are left in the string unchanged, i.e., *the backslash is left in the result*. (This behavior is useful when debugging: if an escape sequence is mistyped, the resulting output is more easily recognized as broken.) It is also important to note that the escape sequences only recognized in string literals fall into the category of unrecognized escapes for bytes literals.

> Changed in version 3.6: Unrecognized escape sequences produce a DeprecationWarning. In some future version of Python they will be a SyntaxError.

Even in a raw literal, quotes can be escaped with a backslash, but the backslash remains in the result; for example, r"\"" is a valid string literal consisting of two characters: a backslash and a double quote; r"\" is not a valid string literal (even a raw string cannot end in an odd number of backslashes). Specifically, *a raw literal cannot end in a single backslash* (since the backslash would escape the following quote character). Note also that a single backslash followed by a newline is interpreted as those two characters as part of the literal, *not* as a line continuation.

---

[1] http://www.unicode.org/Public/9.0.0/ucd/NameAliases.txt

2.4.2 String literal concatenation

Multiple adjacent string or bytes literals (delimited by whitespace), possibly using different quoting conventions, are allowed, and their meaning is the same as their concatenation. Thus, `"hello" 'world'` is equivalent to `"helloworld"`. This feature can be used to reduce the number of backslashes needed, to split long strings conveniently across long lines, or even to add comments to parts of strings, for example:

```
re.compile("[A-Za-z_]"       # letter or underscore
           "[A-Za-z0-9_]*"   # letter, digit or underscore
          )
```

Note that this feature is defined at the syntactical level, but implemented at compile time. The '+' operator must be used to concatenate string expressions at run time. Also note that literal concatenation can use different quoting styles for each component (even mixing raw strings and triple quoted strings), and formatted string literals may be concatenated with plain string literals.

2.4.3 Formatted string literals

New in version 3.6.

A *formatted string literal* or *f-string* is a string literal that is prefixed with `'f'` or `'F'`. These strings may contain replacement fields, which are expressions delimited by curly braces `{}`. While other string literals always have a constant value, formatted strings are really expressions evaluated at run time.

Escape sequences are decoded like in ordinary string literals (except when a literal is also marked as a raw string). After decoding, the grammar for the contents of the string is:

```
f_string          ::=  (literal_char | "{{" | "}}" | replacement_field)*
replacement_field ::=  "{" f_expression ["!" conversion] [":" format_spec] "}"
f_expression      ::=  (conditional_expression | "*" or_expr)
                       ("," conditional_expression | "," "*" or_expr)* [","]
                       | yield_expression
conversion        ::=  "s" | "r" | "a"
format_spec       ::=  (literal_char | NULL | replacement_field)*
literal_char      ::=  <any code point except "{", "}" or NULL>
```

The parts of the string outside curly braces are treated literally, except that any doubled curly braces `'{{'` or `'}}'` are replaced with the corresponding single curly brace. A single opening curly bracket `'{'` marks a replacement field, which starts with a Python expression. After the expression, there may be a conversion field, introduced by an exclamation point `'!'`. A format specifier may also be appended, introduced by a colon `':'`. A replacement field ends with a closing curly bracket `'}'`.

Expressions in formatted string literals are treated like regular Python expressions surrounded by parentheses, with a few exceptions. An empty expression is not allowed, and a *lambda* expression must be surrounded by explicit parentheses. Replacement expressions can contain line breaks (e.g. in triple-quoted strings), but they cannot contain comments. Each expression is evaluated in the context where the formatted string literal appears, in order from left to right.

If a conversion is specified, the result of evaluating the expression is converted before formatting. Conversion `'!s'` calls `str()` on the result, `'!r'` calls `repr()`, and `'!a'` calls `ascii()`.

The result is then formatted using the `format()` protocol. The format specifier is passed to the `__format__()` method of the expression or conversion result. An empty string is passed when the format specifier is omitted. The formatted result is then included in the final value of the whole string.

Top-level format specifiers may include nested replacement fields. These nested fields may include their own conversion fields and format specifiers, but may not include more deeply-nested replacement fields. The format specifier mini-language is the same as that used by the string .format() method.

Formatted string literals may be concatenated, but replacement fields cannot be split across literals.

Some examples of formatted string literals:

```
>>> name = "Fred"
>>> f"He said his name is {name!r}."
"He said his name is 'Fred'."
>>> f"He said his name is {repr(name)}."  # repr() is equivalent to !r
"He said his name is 'Fred'."
>>> width = 10
>>> precision = 4
>>> value = decimal.Decimal("12.34567")
>>> f"result: {value:{width}.{precision}}"  # nested fields
'result:      12.35'
>>> today = datetime(year=2017, month=1, day=27)
>>> f"{today:%B %d, %Y}"  # using date format specifier
'January 27, 2017'
>>> number = 1024
>>> f"{number:#0x}"  # using integer format specifier
'0x400'
```

A consequence of sharing the same syntax as regular string literals is that characters in the replacement fields must not conflict with the quoting used in the outer formatted string literal:

```
f"abc {a["x"]} def"    # error: outer string literal ended prematurely
f"abc {a['x']} def"    # workaround: use different quoting
```

Backslashes are not allowed in format expressions and will raise an error:

```
f"newline: {ord('\n')}"  # raises SyntaxError
```

To include a value in which a backslash escape is required, create a temporary variable.

```
>>> newline = ord('\n')
>>> f"newline: {newline}"
'newline: 10'
```

Formatted string literals cannot be used as docstrings, even if they do not include expressions.

```
>>> def foo():
...     f"Not a docstring"
...
>>> foo.__doc__ is None
True
```

See also PEP 498 for the proposal that added formatted string literals, and str.format(), which uses a related format string mechanism.

2.4.4 Numeric literals

There are three types of numeric literals: integers, floating point numbers, and imaginary numbers. There are no complex literals (complex numbers can be formed by adding a real number and an imaginary number).

Note that numeric literals do not include a sign; a phrase like -1 is actually an expression composed of the unary operator '-' and the literal 1.

2.4.5 Integer literals

Integer literals are described by the following lexical definitions:

```
integer        ::=  decinteger | bininteger | octinteger | hexinteger
decinteger     ::=  nonzerodigit (["_"] digit)* | "0"+ (["_"] "0")*
bininteger     ::=  "0" ("b" | "B") (["_"] bindigit)+
octinteger     ::=  "0" ("o" | "O") (["_"] octdigit)+
hexinteger     ::=  "0" ("x" | "X") (["_"] hexdigit)+
nonzerodigit   ::=  "1"..."9"
digit          ::=  "0"..."9"
bindigit       ::=  "0" | "1"
octdigit       ::=  "0"..."7"
hexdigit       ::=  digit | "a"..."f" | "A"..."F"
```

There is no limit for the length of integer literals apart from what can be stored in available memory.

Underscores are ignored for determining the numeric value of the literal. They can be used to group digits for enhanced readability. One underscore can occur between digits, and after base specifiers like 0x.

Note that leading zeros in a non-zero decimal number are not allowed. This is for disambiguation with C-style octal literals, which Python used before version 3.0.

Some examples of integer literals:

```
7       2147483647                       0o177      0b100110111
3       79228162514264337593543950336    0o377      0xdeadbeef
        100_000_000_000                  0b_1110_0101
```

Changed in version 3.6: Underscores are now allowed for grouping purposes in literals.

2.4.6 Floating point literals

Floating point literals are described by the following lexical definitions:

```
floatnumber    ::=  pointfloat | exponentfloat
pointfloat     ::=  [digitpart] fraction | digitpart "."
exponentfloat  ::=  (digitpart | pointfloat) exponent
digitpart      ::=  digit (["_"] digit)*
fraction       ::=  "." digitpart
exponent       ::=  ("e" | "E") ["+" | "-"] digitpart
```

Note that the integer and exponent parts are always interpreted using radix 10. For example, 077e010 is legal, and denotes the same number as 77e10. The allowed range of floating point literals is implementation-dependent. As in integer literals, underscores are supported for digit grouping.

Some examples of floating point literals:

```
3.14    10.     .001    1e100    3.14e-10    0e0    3.14_15_93
```

Changed in version 3.6: Underscores are now allowed for grouping purposes in literals.

2.4.7 Imaginary literals

Imaginary literals are described by the following lexical definitions:

```
imagnumber   ::=   (floatnumber | digitpart) ("j" | "J")
```

An imaginary literal yields a complex number with a real part of 0.0. Complex numbers are represented as a pair of floating point numbers and have the same restrictions on their range. To create a complex number with a nonzero real part, add a floating point number to it, e.g., (3+4j). Some examples of imaginary literals:

```
3.14j   10.j   10j   .001j   1e100j   3.14e-10j   3.14_15_93j
```

2.5 Operators

The following tokens are operators:

```
+     -     *     **     /     //     %     @
<<    >>    &     |      ^     ~
<     >     <=    >=     ==    !=
```

2.6 Delimiters

The following tokens serve as delimiters in the grammar:

```
(     )     [     ]     {     }
,     :     .     ;     @     =     ->
+=    -=    *=    /=     //=   %=    @=
&=    |=    ^=    >>=    <<=   **=
```

The period can also occur in floating-point and imaginary literals. A sequence of three periods has a special meaning as an ellipsis literal. The second half of the list, the augmented assignment operators, serve lexically as delimiters, but also perform an operation.

The following printing ASCII characters have special meaning as part of other tokens or are otherwise significant to the lexical analyzer:

```
'     "     #     \
```

The following printing ASCII characters are not used in Python. Their occurrence outside string literals and comments is an unconditional error:

```
$     ?     `
```

DATA MODEL

3.1 Objects, values and types

Objects are Python's abstraction for data. All data in a Python program is represented by objects or by relations between objects. (In a sense, and in conformance to Von Neumann's model of a "stored program computer," code is also represented by objects.)

Every object has an identity, a type and a value. An object's *identity* never changes once it has been created; you may think of it as the object's address in memory. The '*is*' operator compares the identity of two objects; the id() function returns an integer representing its identity.

CPython implementation detail: For CPython, id(x) is the memory address where x is stored.

An object's type determines the operations that the object supports (e.g., "does it have a length?") and also defines the possible values for objects of that type. The type() function returns an object's type (which is an object itself). Like its identity, an object's *type* is also unchangeable.[1]

The *value* of some objects can change. Objects whose value can change are said to be *mutable*; objects whose value is unchangeable once they are created are called *immutable*. (The value of an immutable container object that contains a reference to a mutable object can change when the latter's value is changed; however the container is still considered immutable, because the collection of objects it contains cannot be changed. So, immutability is not strictly the same as having an unchangeable value, it is more subtle.) An object's mutability is determined by its type; for instance, numbers, strings and tuples are immutable, while dictionaries and lists are mutable.

Objects are never explicitly destroyed; however, when they become unreachable they may be garbage-collected. An implementation is allowed to postpone garbage collection or omit it altogether — it is a matter of implementation quality how garbage collection is implemented, as long as no objects are collected that are still reachable.

CPython implementation detail: CPython currently uses a reference-counting scheme with (optional) delayed detection of cyclically linked garbage, which collects most objects as soon as they become unreachable, but is not guaranteed to collect garbage containing circular references. See the documentation of the gc module for information on controlling the collection of cyclic garbage. Other implementations act differently and CPython may change. Do not depend on immediate finalization of objects when they become unreachable (so you should always close files explicitly).

Note that the use of the implementation's tracing or debugging facilities may keep objects alive that would normally be collectable. Also note that catching an exception with a '*try...except*' statement may keep objects alive.

Some objects contain references to "external" resources such as open files or windows. It is understood that these resources are freed when the object is garbage-collected, but since garbage collection is not guaranteed to happen, such objects also provide an explicit way to release the external resource, usually a

---

[1] It *is* possible in some cases to change an object's type, under certain controlled conditions. It generally isn't a good idea though, since it can lead to some very strange behaviour if it is handled incorrectly.

`close()` method. Programs are strongly recommended to explicitly close such objects. The '*try…finally*' statement and the '*with*' statement provide convenient ways to do this.

Some objects contain references to other objects; these are called *containers*. Examples of containers are tuples, lists and dictionaries. The references are part of a container's value. In most cases, when we talk about the value of a container, we imply the values, not the identities of the contained objects; however, when we talk about the mutability of a container, only the identities of the immediately contained objects are implied. So, if an immutable container (like a tuple) contains a reference to a mutable object, its value changes if that mutable object is changed.

Types affect almost all aspects of object behavior. Even the importance of object identity is affected in some sense: for immutable types, operations that compute new values may actually return a reference to any existing object with the same type and value, while for mutable objects this is not allowed. E.g., after `a = 1; b = 1`, a and b may or may not refer to the same object with the value one, depending on the implementation, but after `c = []; d = []`, c and d are guaranteed to refer to two different, unique, newly created empty lists. (Note that `c = d = []` assigns the same object to both c and d.)

3.2 The standard type hierarchy

Below is a list of the types that are built into Python. Extension modules (written in C, Java, or other languages, depending on the implementation) can define additional types. Future versions of Python may add types to the type hierarchy (e.g., rational numbers, efficiently stored arrays of integers, etc.), although such additions will often be provided via the standard library instead.

Some of the type descriptions below contain a paragraph listing 'special attributes.' These are attributes that provide access to the implementation and are not intended for general use. Their definition may change in the future.

None This type has a single value. There is a single object with this value. This object is accessed through the built-in name `None`. It is used to signify the absence of a value in many situations, e.g., it is returned from functions that don't explicitly return anything. Its truth value is false.

NotImplemented This type has a single value. There is a single object with this value. This object is accessed through the built-in name `NotImplemented`. Numeric methods and rich comparison methods should return this value if they do not implement the operation for the operands provided. (The interpreter will then try the reflected operation, or some other fallback, depending on the operator.) Its truth value is true.

See implementing-the-arithmetic-operations for more details.

Ellipsis This type has a single value. There is a single object with this value. This object is accessed through the literal `...` or the built-in name `Ellipsis`. Its truth value is true.

numbers.Number These are created by numeric literals and returned as results by arithmetic operators and arithmetic built-in functions. Numeric objects are immutable; once created their value never changes. Python numbers are of course strongly related to mathematical numbers, but subject to the limitations of numerical representation in computers.

Python distinguishes between integers, floating point numbers, and complex numbers:

numbers.Integral These represent elements from the mathematical set of integers (positive and negative).

There are two types of integers:

Integers (`int`)

These represent numbers in an unlimited range, subject to available (virtual) memory only. For the purpose of shift and mask operations, a binary representation is assumed, and negative numbers are represented in a variant of 2's complement which gives the illusion of an infinite string of sign bits extending to the left.

Booleans (`bool`) These represent the truth values False and True. The two objects representing the values `False` and `True` are the only Boolean objects. The Boolean type is a subtype of the integer type, and Boolean values behave like the values 0 and 1, respectively, in almost all contexts, the exception being that when converted to a string, the strings `"False"` or `"True"` are returned, respectively.

The rules for integer representation are intended to give the most meaningful interpretation of shift and mask operations involving negative integers.

`numbers.Real` (`float`) These represent machine-level double precision floating point numbers. You are at the mercy of the underlying machine architecture (and C or Java implementation) for the accepted range and handling of overflow. Python does not support single-precision floating point numbers; the savings in processor and memory usage that are usually the reason for using these are dwarfed by the overhead of using objects in Python, so there is no reason to complicate the language with two kinds of floating point numbers.

`numbers.Complex` (`complex`) These represent complex numbers as a pair of machine-level double precision floating point numbers. The same caveats apply as for floating point numbers. The real and imaginary parts of a complex number z can be retrieved through the read-only attributes `z.real` and `z.imag`.

Sequences These represent finite ordered sets indexed by non-negative numbers. The built-in function `len()` returns the number of items of a sequence. When the length of a sequence is n, the index set contains the numbers 0, 1, ..., n-1. Item i of sequence a is selected by `a[i]`.

Sequences also support slicing: `a[i:j]` selects all items with index k such that $i <= k < j$. When used as an expression, a slice is a sequence of the same type. This implies that the index set is renumbered so that it starts at 0.

Some sequences also support "extended slicing" with a third "step" parameter: `a[i:j:k]` selects all items of a with index x where `x = i + n*k`, $n >= 0$ and $i <= x < j$.

Sequences are distinguished according to their mutability:

Immutable sequences An object of an immutable sequence type cannot change once it is created. (If the object contains references to other objects, these other objects may be mutable and may be changed; however, the collection of objects directly referenced by an immutable object cannot change.)

The following types are immutable sequences:

Strings A string is a sequence of values that represent Unicode code points. All the code points in the range U+0000 – U+10FFFF can be represented in a string. Python doesn't have a `char` type; instead, every code point in the string is represented as a string object with length 1. The built-in function `ord()` converts a code point from its string form to an integer in the range 0 – 10FFFF; `chr()` converts an integer in the range 0 – 10FFFF to the corresponding length 1 string object. `str.encode()` can be used to convert a `str` to `bytes` using the given text encoding, and `bytes.decode()` can be used to achieve the opposite.

Tuples The items of a tuple are arbitrary Python objects. Tuples of two or more items are formed by comma-separated lists of expressions. A tuple of one item (a 'singleton') can be formed by affixing a comma to an expression (an expression by itself does not create a tuple, since parentheses must be usable for grouping of expressions). An empty tuple can be formed by an empty pair of parentheses.

Bytes A bytes object is an immutable array. The items are 8-bit bytes, represented by integers in the range $0 <= x < 256$. Bytes literals (like `b'abc'`) and the built-in `bytes()` constructor can be used to create bytes objects. Also, bytes objects can be decoded to strings via the `decode()` method.

Mutable sequences Mutable sequences can be changed after they are created. The subscription and slicing notations can be used as the target of assignment and *del* (delete) statements.

There are currently two intrinsic mutable sequence types:

Lists The items of a list are arbitrary Python objects. Lists are formed by placing a comma-separated list of expressions in square brackets. (Note that there are no special cases needed to form lists of length 0 or 1.)

Byte Arrays A bytearray object is a mutable array. They are created by the built-in `bytearray()` constructor. Aside from being mutable (and hence unhashable), byte arrays otherwise provide the same interface and functionality as immutable `bytes` objects.

The extension module `array` provides an additional example of a mutable sequence type, as does the `collections` module.

Set types These represent unordered, finite sets of unique, immutable objects. As such, they cannot be indexed by any subscript. However, they can be iterated over, and the built-in function `len()` returns the number of items in a set. Common uses for sets are fast membership testing, removing duplicates from a sequence, and computing mathematical operations such as intersection, union, difference, and symmetric difference.

For set elements, the same immutability rules apply as for dictionary keys. Note that numeric types obey the normal rules for numeric comparison: if two numbers compare equal (e.g., 1 and 1.0), only one of them can be contained in a set.

There are currently two intrinsic set types:

Sets These represent a mutable set. They are created by the built-in `set()` constructor and can be modified afterwards by several methods, such as `add()`.

Frozen sets These represent an immutable set. They are created by the built-in `frozenset()` constructor. As a frozenset is immutable and *hashable*, it can be used again as an element of another set, or as a dictionary key.

Mappings These represent finite sets of objects indexed by arbitrary index sets. The subscript notation `a[k]` selects the item indexed by `k` from the mapping `a`; this can be used in expressions and as the target of assignments or *del* statements. The built-in function `len()` returns the number of items in a mapping.

There is currently a single intrinsic mapping type:

Dictionaries These represent finite sets of objects indexed by nearly arbitrary values. The only types of values not acceptable as keys are values containing lists or dictionaries or other mutable types that are compared by value rather than by object identity, the reason being that the efficient implementation of dictionaries requires a key's hash value to remain constant. Numeric types used for keys obey the normal rules for numeric comparison: if two numbers compare equal (e.g., 1 and 1.0) then they can be used interchangeably to index the same dictionary entry.

Dictionaries are mutable; they can be created by the `{...}` notation (see section *Dictionary displays*).

The extension modules `dbm.ndbm` and `dbm.gnu` provide additional examples of mapping types, as does the `collections` module.

Callable types These are the types to which the function call operation (see section *Calls*) can be applied:

User-defined functions A user-defined function object is created by a function definition (see section *Function definitions*). It should be called with an argument list containing the same number of items as the function's formal parameter list.

Special attributes:

Attribute	Meaning	
__doc__	The function's documentation string, or None if unavailable; not inherited by subclasses	Writable
__name__	The function's name	Writable
__qualname__	The function's *qualified name* New in version 3.3.	Writable
__module__	The name of the module the function was defined in, or None if unavailable.	Writable
__defaults__	A tuple containing default argument values for those arguments that have defaults, or None if no arguments have a default value	Writable
__code__	The code object representing the compiled function body.	Writable
__globals__	A reference to the dictionary that holds the function's global variables — the global namespace of the module in which the function was defined.	Read-only
__dict__	The namespace supporting arbitrary function attributes.	Writable
__closure__	None or a tuple of cells that contain bindings for the function's free variables.	Read-only
__annotations__	A dict containing annotations of parameters. The keys of the dict are the parameter names, and 'return' for the return annotation, if provided.	Writable
__kwdefaults__	A dict containing defaults for keyword-only parameters.	Writable

Most of the attributes labelled "Writable" check the type of the assigned value.

Function objects also support getting and setting arbitrary attributes, which can be used, for example, to attach metadata to functions. Regular attribute dot-notation is used to get and set such attributes. *Note that the current implementation only supports function attributes on user-defined functions. Function attributes on built-in functions may be supported in the future.*

Additional information about a function's definition can be retrieved from its code object; see the description of internal types below.

Instance methods An instance method object combines a class, a class instance and any callable object (normally a user-defined function).

Special read-only attributes: __self__ is the class instance object, __func__ is the function object; __doc__ is the method's documentation (same as __func__.__doc__); __name__ is the method name (same as __func__.__name__); __module__ is the name of the module the method was defined in, or None if unavailable.

Methods also support accessing (but not setting) the arbitrary function attributes on the underlying function object.

User-defined method objects may be created when getting an attribute of a class (perhaps via an instance of that class), if that attribute is a user-defined function object or a class method object.

When an instance method object is created by retrieving a user-defined function object from a class via one of its instances, its __self__ attribute is the instance, and the method object is said to be bound. The new method's __func__ attribute is the original function object.

When a user-defined method object is created by retrieving another method object from a class or instance, the behaviour is the same as for a function object, except that the __func__ attribute of the new instance is not the original method object but its __func__ attribute.

When an instance method object is created by retrieving a class method object from a class or instance, its `__self__` attribute is the class itself, and its `__func__` attribute is the function object underlying the class method.

When an instance method object is called, the underlying function (`__func__`) is called, inserting the class instance (`__self__`) in front of the argument list. For instance, when C is a class which contains a definition for a function f(), and x is an instance of C, calling x.f(1) is equivalent to calling C.f(x, 1).

When an instance method object is derived from a class method object, the "class instance" stored in `__self__` will actually be the class itself, so that calling either x.f(1) or C.f(1) is equivalent to calling f(C,1) where f is the underlying function.

Note that the transformation from function object to instance method object happens each time the attribute is retrieved from the instance. In some cases, a fruitful optimization is to assign the attribute to a local variable and call that local variable. Also notice that this transformation only happens for user-defined functions; other callable objects (and all non-callable objects) are retrieved without transformation. It is also important to note that user-defined functions which are attributes of a class instance are not converted to bound methods; this *only* happens when the function is an attribute of the class.

Generator functions A function or method which uses the *yield* statement (see section *The yield statement*) is called a *generator function*. Such a function, when called, always returns an iterator object which can be used to execute the body of the function: calling the iterator's `iterator.__next__()` method will cause the function to execute until it provides a value using the *yield* statement. When the function executes a *return* statement or falls off the end, a `StopIteration` exception is raised and the iterator will have reached the end of the set of values to be returned.

Coroutine functions A function or method which is defined using *async def* is called a *coroutine function*. Such a function, when called, returns a *coroutine* object. It may contain *await* expressions, as well as *async with* and *async for* statements. See also the *Coroutine Objects* section.

Asynchronous generator functions A function or method which is defined using *async def* and which uses the *yield* statement is called a *asynchronous generator function*. Such a function, when called, returns an asynchronous iterator object which can be used in an *async for* statement to execute the body of the function.

Calling the asynchronous iterator's `aiterator.__anext__()` method will return an *awaitable* which when awaited will execute until it provides a value using the *yield* expression. When the function executes an empty *return* statement or falls off the end, a `StopAsyncIteration` exception is raised and the asynchronous iterator will have reached the end of the set of values to be yielded.

Built-in functions A built-in function object is a wrapper around a C function. Examples of built-in functions are `len()` and `math.sin()` (math is a standard built-in module). The number and type of the arguments are determined by the C function. Special read-only attributes: `__doc__` is the function's documentation string, or `None` if unavailable; `__name__` is the function's name; `__self__` is set to `None` (but see the next item); `__module__` is the name of the module the function was defined in or `None` if unavailable.

Built-in methods This is really a different disguise of a built-in function, this time containing an object passed to the C function as an implicit extra argument. An example of a built-in method is `alist.append()`, assuming *alist* is a list object. In this case, the special read-only attribute `__self__` is set to the object denoted by *alist*.

Classes Classes are callable. These objects normally act as factories for new instances of themselves, but variations are possible for class types that override `__new__()`. The arguments of the call are passed to `__new__()` and, in the typical case, to `__init__()` to initialize the new instance.

Class Instances Instances of arbitrary classes can be made callable by defining a `__call__()` method in their class.

Modules Modules are a basic organizational unit of Python code, and are created by the *import system* as invoked either by the *import* statement (see *import*), or by calling functions such as `importlib.import_module()` and built-in `__import__()`. A module object has a namespace implemented by a dictionary object (this is the dictionary referenced by the `__globals__` attribute of functions defined in the module). Attribute references are translated to lookups in this dictionary, e.g., `m.x` is equivalent to `m.__dict__["x"]`. A module object does not contain the code object used to initialize the module (since it isn't needed once the initialization is done).

Attribute assignment updates the module's namespace dictionary, e.g., `m.x = 1` is equivalent to `m.__dict__["x"] = 1`.

Predefined (writable) attributes: `__name__` is the module's name; `__doc__` is the module's documentation string, or `None` if unavailable; `__annotations__` (optional) is a dictionary containing *variable annotations* collected during module body execution; `__file__` is the pathname of the file from which the module was loaded, if it was loaded from a file. The `__file__` attribute may be missing for certain types of modules, such as C modules that are statically linked into the interpreter; for extension modules loaded dynamically from a shared library, it is the pathname of the shared library file.

Special read-only attribute: `__dict__` is the module's namespace as a dictionary object.

CPython implementation detail: Because of the way CPython clears module dictionaries, the module dictionary will be cleared when the module falls out of scope even if the dictionary still has live references. To avoid this, copy the dictionary or keep the module around while using its dictionary directly.

Custom classes Custom class types are typically created by class definitions (see section *Class definitions*). A class has a namespace implemented by a dictionary object. Class attribute references are translated to lookups in this dictionary, e.g., `C.x` is translated to `C.__dict__["x"]` (although there are a number of hooks which allow for other means of locating attributes). When the attribute name is not found there, the attribute search continues in the base classes. This search of the base classes uses the C3 method resolution order which behaves correctly even in the presence of 'diamond' inheritance structures where there are multiple inheritance paths leading back to a common ancestor. Additional details on the C3 MRO used by Python can be found in the documentation accompanying the 2.3 release at https://www.python.org/download/releases/2.3/mro/.

When a class attribute reference (for class `C`, say) would yield a class method object, it is transformed into an instance method object whose `__self__` attributes is `C`. When it would yield a static method object, it is transformed into the object wrapped by the static method object. See section *Implementing Descriptors* for another way in which attributes retrieved from a class may differ from those actually contained in its `__dict__`.

Class attribute assignments update the class's dictionary, never the dictionary of a base class.

A class object can be called (see above) to yield a class instance (see below).

Special attributes: `__name__` is the class name; `__module__` is the module name in which the class was defined; `__dict__` is the dictionary containing the class's namespace; `__bases__` is a tuple containing the base classes, in the order of their occurrence in the base class list; `__doc__` is the class's documentation string, or `None` if undefined; `__annotations__` (optional) is a dictionary containing *variable annotations* collected during class body execution.

Class instances A class instance is created by calling a class object (see above). A class instance has a namespace implemented as a dictionary which is the first place in which attribute references are searched. When an attribute is not found there, and the instance's class has an attribute by that name, the search continues with the class attributes. If a class attribute is found that is a user-defined function object, it is transformed into an instance method object whose `__self__` attribute is the instance. Static method and class method objects are also transformed; see above under "Classes".

See section *Implementing Descriptors* for another way in which attributes of a class retrieved via its instances may differ from the objects actually stored in the class's `__dict__`. If no class attribute is found, and the object's class has a `__getattr__()` method, that is called to satisfy the lookup.

Attribute assignments and deletions update the instance's dictionary, never a class's dictionary. If the class has a `__setattr__()` or `__delattr__()` method, this is called instead of updating the instance dictionary directly.

Class instances can pretend to be numbers, sequences, or mappings if they have methods with certain special names. See section *Special method names*.

Special attributes: `__dict__` is the attribute dictionary; `__class__` is the instance's class.

I/O objects (also known as file objects) A *file object* represents an open file. Various shortcuts are available to create file objects: the `open()` built-in function, and also `os.popen()`, `os.fdopen()`, and the `makefile()` method of socket objects (and perhaps by other functions or methods provided by extension modules).

The objects `sys.stdin`, `sys.stdout` and `sys.stderr` are initialized to file objects corresponding to the interpreter's standard input, output and error streams; they are all open in text mode and therefore follow the interface defined by the `io.TextIOBase` abstract class.

Internal types A few types used internally by the interpreter are exposed to the user. Their definitions may change with future versions of the interpreter, but they are mentioned here for completeness.

Code objects Code objects represent *byte-compiled* executable Python code, or *bytecode*. The difference between a code object and a function object is that the function object contains an explicit reference to the function's globals (the module in which it was defined), while a code object contains no context; also the default argument values are stored in the function object, not in the code object (because they represent values calculated at run-time). Unlike function objects, code objects are immutable and contain no references (directly or indirectly) to mutable objects.

Special read-only attributes: `co_name` gives the function name; `co_argcount` is the number of positional arguments (including arguments with default values); `co_nlocals` is the number of local variables used by the function (including arguments); `co_varnames` is a tuple containing the names of the local variables (starting with the argument names); `co_cellvars` is a tuple containing the names of local variables that are referenced by nested functions; `co_freevars` is a tuple containing the names of free variables; `co_code` is a string representing the sequence of bytecode instructions; `co_consts` is a tuple containing the literals used by the bytecode; `co_names` is a tuple containing the names used by the bytecode; `co_filename` is the filename from which the code was compiled; `co_firstlineno` is the first line number of the function; `co_lnotab` is a string encoding the mapping from bytecode offsets to line numbers (for details see the source code of the interpreter); `co_stacksize` is the required stack size (including local variables); `co_flags` is an integer encoding a number of flags for the interpreter.

The following flag bits are defined for `co_flags`: bit `0x04` is set if the function uses the `*arguments` syntax to accept an arbitrary number of positional arguments; bit `0x08` is set if the function uses the `**keywords` syntax to accept arbitrary keyword arguments; bit `0x20` is set if the function is a generator.

Future feature declarations (`from __future__ import division`) also use bits in `co_flags` to indicate whether a code object was compiled with a particular feature enabled: bit `0x2000` is set if the function was compiled with future division enabled; bits `0x10` and `0x1000` were used in earlier versions of Python.

Other bits in `co_flags` are reserved for internal use.

If a code object represents a function, the first item in `co_consts` is the documentation string of the function, or `None` if undefined.

Frame objects Frame objects represent execution frames. They may occur in traceback objects (see below).

Special read-only attributes: `f_back` is to the previous stack frame (towards the caller), or `None` if this is the bottom stack frame; `f_code` is the code object being executed in this frame; `f_locals` is the dictionary used to look up local variables; `f_globals` is used for global variables; `f_builtins` is used for built-in (intrinsic) names; `f_lasti` gives the precise instruction (this is an index into the bytecode string of the code object).

Special writable attributes: `f_trace`, if not `None`, is a function called at the start of each source code line (this is used by the debugger); `f_lineno` is the current line number of the frame — writing to this from within a trace function jumps to the given line (only for the bottom-most frame). A debugger can implement a Jump command (aka Set Next Statement) by writing to f_lineno.

Frame objects support one method:

`frame.clear()`

This method clears all references to local variables held by the frame. Also, if the frame belonged to a generator, the generator is finalized. This helps break reference cycles involving frame objects (for example when catching an exception and storing its traceback for later use).

`RuntimeError` is raised if the frame is currently executing.

New in version 3.4.

Traceback objects Traceback objects represent a stack trace of an exception. A traceback object is created when an exception occurs. When the search for an exception handler unwinds the execution stack, at each unwound level a traceback object is inserted in front of the current traceback. When an exception handler is entered, the stack trace is made available to the program. (See section *The try statement*.) It is accessible as the third item of the tuple returned by `sys.exc_info()`. When the program contains no suitable handler, the stack trace is written (nicely formatted) to the standard error stream; if the interpreter is interactive, it is also made available to the user as `sys.last_traceback`.

Special read-only attributes: `tb_next` is the next level in the stack trace (towards the frame where the exception occurred), or `None` if there is no next level; `tb_frame` points to the execution frame of the current level; `tb_lineno` gives the line number where the exception occurred; `tb_lasti` indicates the precise instruction. The line number and last instruction in the traceback may differ from the line number of its frame object if the exception occurred in a *try* statement with no matching except clause or with a finally clause.

Slice objects Slice objects are used to represent slices for `__getitem__()` methods. They are also created by the built-in `slice()` function.

Special read-only attributes: `start` is the lower bound; `stop` is the upper bound; `step` is the step value; each is `None` if omitted. These attributes can have any type.

Slice objects support one method:

`slice.indices`(*self*, *length*)

This method takes a single integer argument *length* and computes information about the slice that the slice object would describe if applied to a sequence of *length* items. It returns a tuple of three integers; respectively these are the *start* and *stop* indices and the *step* or stride length of the slice. Missing or out-of-bounds indices are handled in a manner consistent with regular slices.

Static method objects Static method objects provide a way of defeating the transformation of function objects to method objects described above. A static method object is a wrapper around any other object, usually a user-defined method object. When a static method object is retrieved from a class or a class instance, the object actually returned is the wrapped object, which is not subject to any further transformation. Static method objects are not themselves callable, although the objects they wrap usually are. Static method objects are created by the built-in `staticmethod()` constructor.

Class method objects A class method object, like a static method object, is a wrapper around another object that alters the way in which that object is retrieved from classes and class instances. The behaviour of class method objects upon such retrieval is described above, under "User-defined methods". Class method objects are created by the built-in `classmethod()` constructor.

3.3 Special method names

A class can implement certain operations that are invoked by special syntax (such as arithmetic operations or subscripting and slicing) by defining methods with special names. This is Python's approach to *operator overloading*, allowing classes to define their own behavior with respect to language operators. For instance, if a class defines a method named `__getitem__()`, and x is an instance of this class, then `x[i]` is roughly equivalent to `type(x).__getitem__(x, i)`. Except where mentioned, attempts to execute an operation raise an exception when no appropriate method is defined (typically `AttributeError` or `TypeError`).

Setting a special method to `None` indicates that the corresponding operation is not available. For example, if a class sets `__iter__()` to `None`, the class is not iterable, so calling `iter()` on its instances will raise a `TypeError` (without falling back to `__getitem__()`).[2]

When implementing a class that emulates any built-in type, it is important that the emulation only be implemented to the degree that it makes sense for the object being modelled. For example, some sequences may work well with retrieval of individual elements, but extracting a slice may not make sense. (One example of this is the `NodeList` interface in the W3C's Document Object Model.)

3.3.1 Basic customization

`object.__new__(cls[, ...])`

Called to create a new instance of class *cls*. `__new__()` is a static method (special-cased so you need not declare it as such) that takes the class of which an instance was requested as its first argument. The remaining arguments are those passed to the object constructor expression (the call to the class). The return value of `__new__()` should be the new object instance (usually an instance of *cls*).

Typical implementations create a new instance of the class by invoking the superclass's `__new__()` method using `super().__new__(cls[, ...])` with appropriate arguments and then modifying the newly-created instance as necessary before returning it.

If `__new__()` returns an instance of *cls*, then the new instance's `__init__()` method will be invoked like `__init__(self[, ...])`, where *self* is the new instance and the remaining arguments are the same as were passed to `__new__()`.

If `__new__()` does not return an instance of *cls*, then the new instance's `__init__()` method will not be invoked.

`__new__()` is intended mainly to allow subclasses of immutable types (like int, str, or tuple) to customize instance creation. It is also commonly overridden in custom metaclasses in order to customize class creation.

`object.__init__(self[, ...])`

Called after the instance has been created (by `__new__()`), but before it is returned to the caller. The arguments are those passed to the class constructor expression. If a base class has an `__init__()`

---

[2] The `__hash__()`, `__iter__()`, `__reversed__()`, and `__contains__()` methods have special handling for this; others will still raise a `TypeError`, but may do so by relying on the behavior that `None` is not callable.

method, the derived class's `__init__()` method, if any, must explicitly call it to ensure proper initialization of the base class part of the instance; for example: `super().__init__([args...])`.

Because `__new__()` and `__init__()` work together in constructing objects (`__new__()` to create it, and `__init__()` to customize it), no non-`None` value may be returned by `__init__()`; doing so will cause a `TypeError` to be raised at runtime.

`object.__del__(`*self*`)`

Called when the instance is about to be destroyed. This is also called a finalizer or (improperly) a destructor. If a base class has a `__del__()` method, the derived class's `__del__()` method, if any, must explicitly call it to ensure proper deletion of the base class part of the instance.

It is possible (though not recommended!) for the `__del__()` method to postpone destruction of the instance by creating a new reference to it. This is called object *resurrection*. It is implementation-dependent whether `__del__()` is called a second time when a resurrected object is about to be destroyed; the current *CPython* implementation only calls it once.

It is not guaranteed that `__del__()` methods are called for objects that still exist when the interpreter exits.

Note: `del x` doesn't directly call `x.__del__()` — the former decrements the reference count for `x` by one, and the latter is only called when `x`'s reference count reaches zero.

CPython implementation detail: It is possible for a reference cycle to prevent the reference count of an object from going to zero. In this case, the cycle will be later detected and deleted by the *cyclic garbage collector*. A common cause of reference cycles is when an exception has been caught in a local variable. The frame's locals then reference the exception, which references its own traceback, which references the locals of all frames caught in the traceback.

See also:

Documentation for the `gc` module.

Warning: Due to the precarious circumstances under which `__del__()` methods are invoked, exceptions that occur during their execution are ignored, and a warning is printed to `sys.stderr` instead. In particular:

- `__del__()` can be invoked when arbitrary code is being executed, including from any arbitrary thread. If `__del__()` needs to take a lock or invoke any other blocking resource, it may deadlock as the resource may already be taken by the code that gets interrupted to execute `__del__()`.

- `__del__()` can be executed during interpreter shutdown. As a consequence, the global variables it needs to access (including other modules) may already have been deleted or set to `None`. Python guarantees that globals whose name begins with a single underscore are deleted from their module before other globals are deleted; if no other references to such globals exist, this may help in assuring that imported modules are still available at the time when the `__del__()` method is called.

`object.__repr__(`*self*`)`

Called by the `repr()` built-in function to compute the "official" string representation of an object. If at all possible, this should look like a valid Python expression that could be used to recreate an object with the same value (given an appropriate environment). If this is not possible, a string of the form `<...some useful description...>` should be returned. The return value must be a string object. If a class defines `__repr__()` but not `__str__()`, then `__repr__()` is also used when an "informal" string representation of instances of that class is required.

This is typically used for debugging, so it is important that the representation is information-rich and unambiguous.

object.__str__(*self*)
> Called by str(object) and the built-in functions format() and print() to compute the "informal" or nicely printable string representation of an object. The return value must be a string object.
>
> This method differs from *object.__repr__()* in that there is no expectation that *__str__()* return a valid Python expression: a more convenient or concise representation can be used.
>
> The default implementation defined by the built-in type object calls *object.__repr__()*.

object.__bytes__(*self*)
> Called by bytes to compute a byte-string representation of an object. This should return a bytes object.

object.__format__(*self*, *format_spec*)
> Called by the format() built-in function, and by extension, evaluation of *formatted string literals* and the str.format() method, to produce a "formatted" string representation of an object. The format_spec argument is a string that contains a description of the formatting options desired. The interpretation of the format_spec argument is up to the type implementing *__format__()*, however most classes will either delegate formatting to one of the built-in types, or use a similar formatting option syntax.
>
> See formatspec for a description of the standard formatting syntax.
>
> The return value must be a string object.
>
> Changed in version 3.4: The __format__ method of object itself raises a TypeError if passed any non-empty string.

object.__lt__(*self*, *other*)
object.__le__(*self*, *other*)
object.__eq__(*self*, *other*)
object.__ne__(*self*, *other*)
object.__gt__(*self*, *other*)
object.__ge__(*self*, *other*)
> These are the so-called "rich comparison" methods. The correspondence between operator symbols and method names is as follows: x<y calls x.__lt__(y), x<=y calls x.__le__(y), x==y calls x.__eq__(y), x!=y calls x.__ne__(y), x>y calls x.__gt__(y), and x>=y calls x.__ge__(y).
>
> A rich comparison method may return the singleton NotImplemented if it does not implement the operation for a given pair of arguments. By convention, False and True are returned for a successful comparison. However, these methods can return any value, so if the comparison operator is used in a Boolean context (e.g., in the condition of an if statement), Python will call bool() on the value to determine if the result is true or false.
>
> By default, *__ne__()* delegates to *__eq__()* and inverts the result unless it is NotImplemented. There are no other implied relationships among the comparison operators, for example, the truth of (x<y or x==y) does not imply x<=y. To automatically generate ordering operations from a single root operation, see functools.total_ordering().
>
> See the paragraph on *__hash__()* for some important notes on creating *hashable* objects which support custom comparison operations and are usable as dictionary keys.
>
> There are no swapped-argument versions of these methods (to be used when the left argument does not support the operation but the right argument does); rather, *__lt__()* and *__gt__()* are each other's reflection, *__le__()* and *__ge__()* are each other's reflection, and *__eq__()* and *__ne__()* are their own reflection. If the operands are of different types, and right operand's type is a direct or indirect subclass of the left operand's type, the reflected method of the right operand has priority, otherwise the left operand's method has priority. Virtual subclassing is not considered.

`object.__hash__`(*self*)

Called by built-in function `hash()` and for operations on members of hashed collections including `set`, `frozenset`, and `dict`. `__hash__`() should return an integer. The only required property is that objects which compare equal have the same hash value; it is advised to mix together the hash values of the components of the object that also play a part in comparison of objects by packing them into a tuple and hashing the tuple. Example:

```
def __hash__(self):
    return hash((self.name, self.nick, self.color))
```

Note: `hash()` truncates the value returned from an object's custom `__hash__`() method to the size of a `Py_ssize_t`. This is typically 8 bytes on 64-bit builds and 4 bytes on 32-bit builds. If an object's `__hash__`() must interoperate on builds of different bit sizes, be sure to check the width on all supported builds. An easy way to do this is with `python -c "import sys; print(sys.hash_info.width)"`.

If a class does not define an `__eq__`() method it should not define a `__hash__`() operation either; if it defines `__eq__`() but not `__hash__`(), its instances will not be usable as items in hashable collections. If a class defines mutable objects and implements an `__eq__`() method, it should not implement `__hash__`(), since the implementation of hashable collections requires that a key's hash value is immutable (if the object's hash value changes, it will be in the wrong hash bucket).

User-defined classes have `__eq__`() and `__hash__`() methods by default; with them, all objects compare unequal (except with themselves) and `x.__hash__`() returns an appropriate value such that `x == y` implies both that `x is y` and `hash(x) == hash(y)`.

A class that overrides `__eq__`() and does not define `__hash__`() will have its `__hash__`() implicitly set to `None`. When the `__hash__`() method of a class is `None`, instances of the class will raise an appropriate `TypeError` when a program attempts to retrieve their hash value, and will also be correctly identified as unhashable when checking `isinstance(obj, collections.Hashable)`.

If a class that overrides `__eq__`() needs to retain the implementation of `__hash__`() from a parent class, the interpreter must be told this explicitly by setting `__hash__ = <ParentClass>.__hash__`.

If a class that does not override `__eq__`() wishes to suppress hash support, it should include `__hash__ = None` in the class definition. A class which defines its own `__hash__`() that explicitly raises a `TypeError` would be incorrectly identified as hashable by an `isinstance(obj, collections.Hashable)` call.

Note: By default, the `__hash__`() values of str, bytes and datetime objects are "salted" with an unpredictable random value. Although they remain constant within an individual Python process, they are not predictable between repeated invocations of Python.

This is intended to provide protection against a denial-of-service caused by carefully-chosen inputs that exploit the worst case performance of a dict insertion, O(n^2) complexity. See http://www.ocert.org/advisories/ocert-2011-003.html for details.

Changing hash values affects the iteration order of dicts, sets and other mappings. Python has never made guarantees about this ordering (and it typically varies between 32-bit and 64-bit builds).

See also `PYTHONHASHSEED`.

Changed in version 3.3: Hash randomization is enabled by default.

`object.__bool__`(*self*)

Called to implement truth value testing and the built-in operation `bool()`; should return `False` or `True`. When this method is not defined, `__len__`() is called, if it is defined, and the object is considered true if its result is nonzero. If a class defines neither *__len__* () nor *__bool__* (), all its instances are considered true.

3.3.2 Customizing attribute access

The following methods can be defined to customize the meaning of attribute access (use of, assignment to, or deletion of **x.name**) for class instances.

object.**__getattr__**(*self*, *name*)

Called when an attribute lookup has not found the attribute in the usual places (i.e. it is not an instance attribute nor is it found in the class tree for **self**). **name** is the attribute name. This method should return the (computed) attribute value or raise an **AttributeError** exception.

Note that if the attribute is found through the normal mechanism, *__getattr__* () is not called. (This is an intentional asymmetry between *__getattr__* () and *__setattr__* ().) This is done both for efficiency reasons and because otherwise *__getattr__* () would have no way to access other attributes of the instance. Note that at least for instance variables, you can fake total control by not inserting any values in the instance attribute dictionary (but instead inserting them in another object). See the *__getattribute__* () method below for a way to actually get total control over attribute access.

object.**__getattribute__**(*self*, *name*)

Called unconditionally to implement attribute accesses for instances of the class. If the class also defines *__getattr__* (), the latter will not be called unless *__getattribute__* () either calls it explicitly or raises an **AttributeError**. This method should return the (computed) attribute value or raise an **AttributeError** exception. In order to avoid infinite recursion in this method, its implementation should always call the base class method with the same name to access any attributes it needs, for example, object.**__getattribute__**(self, name).

Note: This method may still be bypassed when looking up special methods as the result of implicit invocation via language syntax or built-in functions. See *Special method lookup*.

---

object.**__setattr__**(*self*, *name*, *value*)

Called when an attribute assignment is attempted. This is called instead of the normal mechanism (i.e. store the value in the instance dictionary). *name* is the attribute name, *value* is the value to be assigned to it.

If *__setattr__* () wants to assign to an instance attribute, it should call the base class method with the same name, for example, object.**__setattr__**(self, name, value).

object.**__delattr__**(*self*, *name*)

Like *__setattr__* () but for attribute deletion instead of assignment. This should only be implemented if **del obj.name** is meaningful for the object.

object.**__dir__**(*self*)

Called when **dir()** is called on the object. A sequence must be returned. **dir()** converts the returned sequence to a list and sorts it.

Customizing module attribute access

For a more fine grained customization of the module behavior (setting attributes, properties, etc.), one can set the **__class__** attribute of a module object to a subclass of **types.ModuleType**. For example:

```
import sys
from types import ModuleType

class VerboseModule(ModuleType):
```

```
    def __repr__(self):
        return f'Verbose {self.__name__}'

    def __setattr__(self, attr, value):
        print(f'Setting {attr}...')
        setattr(self, attr, value)

sys.modules[__name__].__class__ = VerboseModule
```

Note: Setting module `__class__` only affects lookups made using the attribute access syntax – directly accessing the module globals (whether by code within the module, or via a reference to the module's globals dictionary) is unaffected.

Changed in version 3.5: `__class__` module attribute is now writable.

Implementing Descriptors

The following methods only apply when an instance of the class containing the method (a so-called *descriptor* class) appears in an *owner* class (the descriptor must be in either the owner's class dictionary or in the class dictionary for one of its parents). In the examples below, "the attribute" refers to the attribute whose name is the key of the property in the owner class' `__dict__`.

`object.__get__`(*self, instance, owner*)
> Called to get the attribute of the owner class (class attribute access) or of an instance of that class (instance attribute access). *owner* is always the owner class, while *instance* is the instance that the attribute was accessed through, or `None` when the attribute is accessed through the *owner*. This method should return the (computed) attribute value or raise an `AttributeError` exception.

`object.__set__`(*self, instance, value*)
> Called to set the attribute on an instance *instance* of the owner class to a new value, *value*.

`object.__delete__`(*self, instance*)
> Called to delete the attribute on an instance *instance* of the owner class.

`object.__set_name__`(*self, owner, name*)
> Called at the time the owning class *owner* is created. The descriptor has been assigned to *name*.

> New in version 3.6.

The attribute `__objclass__` is interpreted by the `inspect` module as specifying the class where this object was defined (setting this appropriately can assist in runtime introspection of dynamic class attributes). For callables, it may indicate that an instance of the given type (or a subclass) is expected or required as the first positional argument (for example, CPython sets this attribute for unbound methods that are implemented in C).

Invoking Descriptors

In general, a descriptor is an object attribute with "binding behavior", one whose attribute access has been overridden by methods in the descriptor protocol: `__get__`(), `__set__`(), and `__delete__`(). If any of those methods are defined for an object, it is said to be a descriptor.

The default behavior for attribute access is to get, set, or delete the attribute from an object's dictionary. For instance, `a.x` has a lookup chain starting with `a.__dict__['x']`, then `type(a).__dict__['x']`, and continuing through the base classes of `type(a)` excluding metaclasses.

However, if the looked-up value is an object defining one of the descriptor methods, then Python may override the default behavior and invoke the descriptor method instead. Where this occurs in the precedence chain depends on which descriptor methods were defined and how they were called.

The starting point for descriptor invocation is a binding, `a.x`. How the arguments are assembled depends on `a`:

Direct Call The simplest and least common call is when user code directly invokes a descriptor method: `x.__get__(a)`.

Instance Binding If binding to an object instance, `a.x` is transformed into the call: `type(a).__dict__['x'].__get__(a, type(a))`.

Class Binding If binding to a class, `A.x` is transformed into the call: `A.__dict__['x'].__get__(None, A)`.

Super Binding If `a` is an instance of `super`, then the binding `super(B, obj).m()` searches `obj.__class__.__mro__` for the base class `A` immediately preceding `B` and then invokes the descriptor with the call: `A.__dict__['m'].__get__(obj, obj.__class__)`.

For instance bindings, the precedence of descriptor invocation depends on the which descriptor methods are defined. A descriptor can define any combination of `__get__()`, `__set__()` and `__delete__()`. If it does not define `__get__()`, then accessing the attribute will return the descriptor object itself unless there is a value in the object's instance dictionary. If the descriptor defines `__set__()` and/or `__delete__()`, it is a data descriptor; if it defines neither, it is a non-data descriptor. Normally, data descriptors define both `__get__()` and `__set__()`, while non-data descriptors have just the `__get__()` method. Data descriptors with `__set__()` and `__get__()` defined always override a redefinition in an instance dictionary. In contrast, non-data descriptors can be overridden by instances.

Python methods (including `staticmethod()` and `classmethod()`) are implemented as non-data descriptors. Accordingly, instances can redefine and override methods. This allows individual instances to acquire behaviors that differ from other instances of the same class.

The `property()` function is implemented as a data descriptor. Accordingly, instances cannot override the behavior of a property.

__slots__

By default, instances of classes have a dictionary for attribute storage. This wastes space for objects having very few instance variables. The space consumption can become acute when creating large numbers of instances.

The default can be overridden by defining *__slots__* in a class definition. The *__slots__* declaration takes a sequence of instance variables and reserves just enough space in each instance to hold a value for each variable. Space is saved because *__dict__* is not created for each instance.

`object.__slots__`
> This class variable can be assigned a string, iterable, or sequence of strings with variable names used by instances. *__slots__* reserves space for the declared variables and prevents the automatic creation of *__dict__* and *__weakref__* for each instance.

Notes on using *__slots__*

- When inheriting from a class without *__slots__*, the *__dict__* attribute of that class will always be accessible, so a *__slots__* definition in the subclass is meaningless.

- Without a *__dict__* variable, instances cannot be assigned new variables not listed in the *__slots__* definition. Attempts to assign to an unlisted variable name raises `AttributeError`. If dynamic assignment of new variables is desired, then add `'__dict__'` to the sequence of strings in the ___*slots*___ declaration.

- Without a ___*weakref*___ variable for each instance, classes defining ___*slots*___ do not support weak references to its instances. If weak reference support is needed, then add `'__weakref__'` to the sequence of strings in the ___*slots*___ declaration.

- ___*slots*___ are implemented at the class level by creating descriptors (*Implementing Descriptors*) for each variable name. As a result, class attributes cannot be used to set default values for instance variables defined by ___*slots*___; otherwise, the class attribute would overwrite the descriptor assignment.

- The action of a ___*slots*___ declaration is limited to the class where it is defined. As a result, subclasses will have a ___*dict*___ unless they also define ___*slots*___ (which must only contain names of any *additional* slots).

- If a class defines a slot also defined in a base class, the instance variable defined by the base class slot is inaccessible (except by retrieving its descriptor directly from the base class). This renders the meaning of the program undefined. In the future, a check may be added to prevent this.

- Nonempty ___*slots*___ does not work for classes derived from "variable-length" built-in types such as `int`, `bytes` and `tuple`.

- Any non-string iterable may be assigned to ___*slots*___. Mappings may also be used; however, in the future, special meaning may be assigned to the values corresponding to each key.

- ___*class*___ assignment works only if both classes have the same ___*slots*___.

3.3.3 Customizing class creation

Whenever a class inherits from another class, ___*init_subclass*___ is called on that class. This way, it is possible to write classes which change the behavior of subclasses. This is closely related to class decorators, but where class decorators only affect the specific class they're applied to, `__init_subclass__` solely applies to future subclasses of the class defining the method.

classmethod object.`__init_subclass__`(*cls*)
> This method is called whenever the containing class is subclassed. *cls* is then the new subclass. If defined as a normal instance method, this method is implicitly converted to a class method.
>
> Keyword arguments which are given to a new class are passed to the parent's class `__init_subclass__`. For compatibility with other classes using `__init_subclass__`, one should take out the needed keyword arguments and pass the others over to the base class, as in:

```
class Philosopher:
    def __init_subclass__(cls, default_name, **kwargs):
        super().__init_subclass__(**kwargs)
        cls.default_name = default_name

class AustralianPhilosopher(Philosopher, default_name="Bruce"):
    pass
```

> The default implementation `object.__init_subclass__` does nothing, but raises an error if it is called with any arguments.

> **Note:** The metaclass hint `metaclass` is consumed by the rest of the type machinery, and is never passed to `__init_subclass__` implementations. The actual metaclass (rather than the explicit hint) can be accessed as `type(cls)`.

> New in version 3.6.

Metaclasses

By default, classes are constructed using `type()`. The class body is executed in a new namespace and the class name is bound locally to the result of `type(name, bases, namespace)`.

The class creation process can be customized by passing the `metaclass` keyword argument in the class definition line, or by inheriting from an existing class that included such an argument. In the following example, both `MyClass` and `MySubclass` are instances of `Meta`:

```
class Meta(type):
    pass

class MyClass(metaclass=Meta):
    pass

class MySubclass(MyClass):
    pass
```

Any other keyword arguments that are specified in the class definition are passed through to all metaclass operations described below.

When a class definition is executed, the following steps occur:

- the appropriate metaclass is determined
- the class namespace is prepared
- the class body is executed
- the class object is created

Determining the appropriate metaclass

The appropriate metaclass for a class definition is determined as follows:

- if no bases and no explicit metaclass are given, then `type()` is used
- if an explicit metaclass is given and it is *not* an instance of `type()`, then it is used directly as the metaclass
- if an instance of `type()` is given as the explicit metaclass, or bases are defined, then the most derived metaclass is used

The most derived metaclass is selected from the explicitly specified metaclass (if any) and the metaclasses (i.e. `type(cls)`) of all specified base classes. The most derived metaclass is one which is a subtype of *all* of these candidate metaclasses. If none of the candidate metaclasses meets that criterion, then the class definition will fail with `TypeError`.

Preparing the class namespace

Once the appropriate metaclass has been identified, then the class namespace is prepared. If the metaclass has a `__prepare__` attribute, it is called as `namespace = metaclass.__prepare__(name, bases, **kwds)` (where the additional keyword arguments, if any, come from the class definition).

If the metaclass has no `__prepare__` attribute, then the class namespace is initialised as an empty ordered mapping.

See also:

PEP 3115 - **Metaclasses in Python 3000** Introduced the `__prepare__` namespace hook

Executing the class body

The class body is executed (approximately) as `exec(body, globals(), namespace)`. The key difference from a normal call to `exec()` is that lexical scoping allows the class body (including any methods) to reference names from the current and outer scopes when the class definition occurs inside a function.

However, even when the class definition occurs inside the function, methods defined inside the class still cannot see names defined at the class scope. Class variables must be accessed through the first parameter of instance or class methods, or through the implicit lexically scoped `__class__` reference described in the next section.

Creating the class object

Once the class namespace has been populated by executing the class body, the class object is created by calling `metaclass(name, bases, namespace, **kwds)` (the additional keywords passed here are the same as those passed to `__prepare__`).

This class object is the one that will be referenced by the zero-argument form of `super()`. `__class__` is an implicit closure reference created by the compiler if any methods in a class body refer to either `__class__` or `super`. This allows the zero argument form of `super()` to correctly identify the class being defined based on lexical scoping, while the class or instance that was used to make the current call is identified based on the first argument passed to the method.

CPython implementation detail: In CPython 3.6 and later, the `__class__` cell is passed to the metaclass as a `__classcell__` entry in the class namespace. If present, this must be propagated up to the `type.__new__` call in order for the class to be initialised correctly. Failing to do so will result in a `DeprecationWarning` in Python 3.6, and a `RuntimeWarning` in the future.

When using the default metaclass `type`, or any metaclass that ultimately calls `type.__new__`, the following additional customisation steps are invoked after creating the class object:

* first, `type.__new__` collects all of the descriptors in the class namespace that define a _`__set_name__`_ _()_ method;
* second, all of these `__set_name__` methods are called with the class being defined and the assigned name of that particular descriptor; and
* finally, the _`__init_subclass__`_ _()_ hook is called on the immediate parent of the new class in its method resolution order.

After the class object is created, it is passed to the class decorators included in the class definition (if any) and the resulting object is bound in the local namespace as the defined class.

When a new class is created by `type.__new__`, the object provided as the namespace parameter is copied to a new ordered mapping and the original object is discarded. The new copy is wrapped in a read-only proxy, which becomes the `__dict__` attribute of the class object.

See also:

PEP 3135 - **New super** Describes the implicit `__class__` closure reference

Metaclass example

The potential uses for metaclasses are boundless. Some ideas that have been explored include enum, logging, interface checking, automatic delegation, automatic property creation, proxies, frameworks, and automatic resource locking/synchronization.

Here is an example of a metaclass that uses an `collections.OrderedDict` to remember the order that class variables are defined:

```
class OrderedClass(type):

    @classmethod
    def __prepare__(metacls, name, bases, **kwds):
        return collections.OrderedDict()

    def __new__(cls, name, bases, namespace, **kwds):
        result = type.__new__(cls, name, bases, dict(namespace))
        result.members = tuple(namespace)
        return result

class A(metaclass=OrderedClass):
    def one(self): pass
    def two(self): pass
    def three(self): pass
    def four(self): pass

>>> A.members
('__module__', 'one', 'two', 'three', 'four')
```

When the class definition for *A* gets executed, the process begins with calling the metaclass's `__prepare__()`
method which returns an empty `collections.OrderedDict`. That mapping records the methods and attributes of *A* as they are defined within the body of the class statement. Once those definitions are executed,
the ordered dictionary is fully populated and the metaclass's *__new__*() method gets invoked. That method
builds the new type and it saves the ordered dictionary keys in an attribute called `members`.

3.3.4 Customizing instance and subclass checks

The following methods are used to override the default behavior of the `isinstance()` and `issubclass()`
built-in functions.

In particular, the metaclass `abc.ABCMeta` implements these methods in order to allow the addition of Abstract
Base Classes (ABCs) as "virtual base classes" to any class or type (including built-in types), including other
ABCs.

`class.__instancecheck__`(*self, instance*)

 Return true if *instance* should be considered a (direct or indirect) instance of *class*. If defined, called
 to implement `isinstance(instance, class)`.

`class.__subclasscheck__`(*self, subclass*)

 Return true if *subclass* should be considered a (direct or indirect) subclass of *class*. If defined, called
 to implement `issubclass(subclass, class)`.

Note that these methods are looked up on the type (metaclass) of a class. They cannot be defined as
class methods in the actual class. This is consistent with the lookup of special methods that are called on
instances, only in this case the instance is itself a class.

See also:

PEP 3119 - **Introducing Abstract Base Classes** Includes the specification for customiz-
 ing `isinstance()` and `issubclass()` behavior through *__instancecheck__*() and
 __subclasscheck__(), with motivation for this functionality in the context of adding Abstract
 Base Classes (see the `abc` module) to the language.

3.3.5 Emulating callable objects

object.__call__(*self*[, *args...*])

    Called when the instance is "called" as a function; if this method is defined, x(arg1, arg2, ...) is a shorthand for x.__call__(arg1, arg2, ...).

3.3.6 Emulating container types

The following methods can be defined to implement container objects. Containers usually are sequences (such as lists or tuples) or mappings (like dictionaries), but can represent other containers as well. The first set of methods is used either to emulate a sequence or to emulate a mapping; the difference is that for a sequence, the allowable keys should be the integers k for which $0 <= k < N$ where N is the length of the sequence, or slice objects, which define a range of items. It is also recommended that mappings provide the methods keys(), values(), items(), get(), clear(), setdefault(), pop(), popitem(), copy(), and update() behaving similar to those for Python's standard dictionary objects. The collections module provides a MutableMapping abstract base class to help create those methods from a base set of __getitem__(), __setitem__(), __delitem__(), and keys(). Mutable sequences should provide methods append(), count(), index(), extend(), insert(), pop(), remove(), reverse() and sort(), like Python standard list objects. Finally, sequence types should implement addition (meaning concatenation) and multiplication (meaning repetition) by defining the methods __add__(), __radd__(), __iadd__(), __mul__(), __rmul__() and __imul__() described below; they should not define other numerical operators. It is recommended that both mappings and sequences implement the __contains__() method to allow efficient use of the in operator; for mappings, in should search the mapping's keys; for sequences, it should search through the values. It is further recommended that both mappings and sequences implement the __iter__() method to allow efficient iteration through the container; for mappings, __iter__() should be the same as keys(); for sequences, it should iterate through the values.

object.__len__(*self*)

    Called to implement the built-in function len(). Should return the length of the object, an integer >= 0. Also, an object that doesn't define a __bool__() method and whose __len__() method returns zero is considered to be false in a Boolean context.

    CPython implementation detail: In CPython, the length is required to be at most sys.maxsize. If the length is larger than sys.maxsize some features (such as len()) may raise OverflowError. To prevent raising OverflowError by truth value testing, an object must define a __bool__() method.

object.__length_hint__(*self*)

    Called to implement operator.length_hint(). Should return an estimated length for the object (which may be greater or less than the actual length). The length must be an integer >= 0. This method is purely an optimization and is never required for correctness.

    New in version 3.4.

Note: Slicing is done exclusively with the following three methods. A call like

```
a[1:2] = b
```

is translated to

```
a[slice(1, 2, None)] = b
```

and so forth. Missing slice items are always filled in with None.

---

object.__getitem__(*self*, *key*)

    Called to implement evaluation of self[key]. For sequence types, the accepted keys should be integers

---

and slice objects. Note that the special interpretation of negative indexes (if the class wishes to emulate a sequence type) is up to the *__getitem__ ()* method. If *key* is of an inappropriate type, TypeError may be raised; if of a value outside the set of indexes for the sequence (after any special interpretation of negative values), IndexError should be raised. For mapping types, if *key* is missing (not in the container), KeyError should be raised.

Note: *for* loops expect that an IndexError will be raised for illegal indexes to allow proper detection of the end of the sequence.

---

object.**__missing__**(*self, key*)
> Called by dict.*__getitem__ ()* to implement self[key] for dict subclasses when key is not in the dictionary.

object.**__setitem__**(*self, key, value*)
> Called to implement assignment to self[key]. Same note as for *__getitem__ ()*. This should only be implemented for mappings if the objects support changes to the values for keys, or if new keys can be added, or for sequences if elements can be replaced. The same exceptions should be raised for improper *key* values as for the *__getitem__ ()* method.

object.**__delitem__**(*self, key*)
> Called to implement deletion of self[key]. Same note as for *__getitem__ ()*. This should only be implemented for mappings if the objects support removal of keys, or for sequences if elements can be removed from the sequence. The same exceptions should be raised for improper *key* values as for the *__getitem__ ()* method.

object.**__iter__**(*self*)
> This method is called when an iterator is required for a container. This method should return a new iterator object that can iterate over all the objects in the container. For mappings, it should iterate over the keys of the container.

> Iterator objects also need to implement this method; they are required to return themselves. For more information on iterator objects, see typeiter.

object.**__reversed__**(*self*)
> Called (if present) by the reversed() built-in to implement reverse iteration. It should return a new iterator object that iterates over all the objects in the container in reverse order.

> If the *__reversed__ ()* method is not provided, the reversed() built-in will fall back to using the sequence protocol (*__len__ ()* and *__getitem__ ()*). Objects that support the sequence protocol should only provide *__reversed__ ()* if they can provide an implementation that is more efficient than the one provided by reversed().

The membership test operators (*in* and *not in*) are normally implemented as an iteration through a sequence. However, container objects can supply the following special method with a more efficient implementation, which also does not require the object be a sequence.

object.**__contains__**(*self, item*)
> Called to implement membership test operators. Should return true if *item* is in *self*, false otherwise. For mapping objects, this should consider the keys of the mapping rather than the values or the key-item pairs.

> For objects that don't define *__contains__ ()*, the membership test first tries iteration via *__iter__ ()*, then the old sequence iteration protocol via *__getitem__ ()*, see *this section in the language reference*.

3.3.7 Emulating numeric types

The following methods can be defined to emulate numeric objects. Methods corresponding to operations that are not supported by the particular kind of number implemented (e.g., bitwise operations for non-integral

---

numbers) should be left undefined.

object.__add__(*self*, *other*)
object.__sub__(*self*, *other*)
object.__mul__(*self*, *other*)
object.__matmul__(*self*, *other*)
object.__truediv__(*self*, *other*)
object.__floordiv__(*self*, *other*)
object.__mod__(*self*, *other*)
object.__divmod__(*self*, *other*)
object.__pow__(*self*, *other*[, *modulo*])
object.__lshift__(*self*, *other*)
object.__rshift__(*self*, *other*)
object.__and__(*self*, *other*)
object.__xor__(*self*, *other*)
object.__or__(*self*, *other*)

> These methods are called to implement the binary arithmetic operations (+, -, *, @, /, //, %, divmod(),
> pow(), **, <<, >>, &, ^, |). For instance, to evaluate the expression x + y, where *x* is an instance of a
> class that has an *__add__*() method, x.__add__(y) is called. The *__divmod__*() method should be
> the equivalent to using *__floordiv__*() and *__mod__*(); it should not be related to *__truediv__*().
> Note that *__pow__*() should be defined to accept an optional third argument if the ternary version of
> the built-in pow() function is to be supported.

> If one of those methods does not support the operation with the supplied arguments, it should return
> NotImplemented.

object.__radd__(*self*, *other*)
object.__rsub__(*self*, *other*)
object.__rmul__(*self*, *other*)
object.__rmatmul__(*self*, *other*)
object.__rtruediv__(*self*, *other*)
object.__rfloordiv__(*self*, *other*)
object.__rmod__(*self*, *other*)
object.__rdivmod__(*self*, *other*)
object.__rpow__(*self*, *other*)
object.__rlshift__(*self*, *other*)
object.__rrshift__(*self*, *other*)
object.__rand__(*self*, *other*)
object.__rxor__(*self*, *other*)
object.__ror__(*self*, *other*)

> These methods are called to implement the binary arithmetic operations (+, -, *, @, /, //, %, divmod(),
> pow(), **, <<, >>, &, ^, |) with reflected (swapped) operands. These functions are only called if the left
> operand does not support the corresponding operation[3] and the operands are of different types.[4] For
> instance, to evaluate the expression x - y, where *y* is an instance of a class that has an *__rsub__*()
> method, y.__rsub__(x) is called if x.__sub__(y) returns *NotImplemented*.

> Note that ternary pow() will not try calling *__rpow__*() (the coercion rules would become too com-
> plicated).

> **Note:** If the right operand's type is a subclass of the left operand's type and that subclass provides
> the reflected method for the operation, this method will be called before the left operand's non-reflected

---

[3] "Does not support" here means that the class has no such method, or the method returns NotImplemented. Do not set the
method to None if you want to force fallback to the right operand's reflected method—that will instead have the opposite effect
of explicitly *blocking* such fallback.

[4] For operands of the same type, it is assumed that if the non-reflected method (such as *__add__*()) fails the operation is
not supported, which is why the reflected method is not called.

---

method. This behavior allows subclasses to override their ancestors' operations.

object.__**iadd**__(*self, other*)
object.__**isub**__(*self, other*)
object.__**imul**__(*self, other*)
object.__**imatmul**__(*self, other*)
object.__**itruediv**__(*self, other*)
object.__**ifloordiv**__(*self, other*)
object.__**imod**__(*self, other*)
object.__**ipow**__(*self, other*[, *modulo*])
object.__**ilshift**__(*self, other*)
object.__**irshift**__(*self, other*)
object.__**iand**__(*self, other*)
object.__**ixor**__(*self, other*)
object.__**ior**__(*self, other*)

These methods are called to implement the augmented arithmetic assignments (+=, -=, *=, @=, /=, //=, %=, **=, <<=, >>=, &=, ^=, |=). These methods should attempt to do the operation in-place (modifying *self*) and return the result (which could be, but does not have to be, *self*). If a specific method is not defined, the augmented assignment falls back to the normal methods. For instance, if x is an instance of a class with an *__iadd__()* method, x += y is equivalent to x = x.__iadd__(y) . Otherwise, x.__add__(y) and y.__radd__(x) are considered, as with the evaluation of x + y. In certain situations, augmented assignment can result in unexpected errors (see faq-augmented-assignment-tuple-error), but this behavior is in fact part of the data model.

object.__**neg**__(*self*)
object.__**pos**__(*self*)
object.__**abs**__(*self*)
object.__**invert**__(*self*)

Called to implement the unary arithmetic operations (-, +, abs() and ~).

object.__**complex**__(*self*)
object.__**int**__(*self*)
object.__**float**__(*self*)
object.__**round**__(*self*[, *n*])

Called to implement the built-in functions complex(), int(), float() and round(). Should return a value of the appropriate type.

object.__**index**__(*self*)

Called to implement operator.index(), and whenever Python needs to losslessly convert the numeric object to an integer object (such as in slicing, or in the built-in bin(), hex() and oct() functions). Presence of this method indicates that the numeric object is an integer type. Must return an integer.

Note: In order to have a coherent integer type class, when *__index__()* is defined *__int__()* should also be defined, and both should return the same value.

3.3.8 With Statement Context Managers

A *context manager* is an object that defines the runtime context to be established when executing a *with* statement. The context manager handles the entry into, and the exit from, the desired runtime context for the execution of the block of code. Context managers are normally invoked using the *with* statement (described in section *The with statement*), but can also be used by directly invoking their methods.

Typical uses of context managers include saving and restoring various kinds of global state, locking and unlocking resources, closing opened files, etc.

For more information on context managers, see typecontextmanager.

object.__enter__(*self*)

> Enter the runtime context related to this object. The *with* statement will bind this method's return value to the target(s) specified in the *as* clause of the statement, if any.

object.__exit__(*self*, *exc_type*, *exc_value*, *traceback*)

> Exit the runtime context related to this object. The parameters describe the exception that caused the context to be exited. If the context was exited without an exception, all three arguments will be None.
>
> If an exception is supplied, and the method wishes to suppress the exception (i.e., prevent it from being propagated), it should return a true value. Otherwise, the exception will be processed normally upon exit from this method.
>
> Note that *__exit__*() methods should not reraise the passed-in exception; this is the caller's responsibility.

See also:

PEP 343 - **The "with" statement** The specification, background, and examples for the Python *with* statement.

3.3.9 Special method lookup

For custom classes, implicit invocations of special methods are only guaranteed to work correctly if defined on an object's type, not in the object's instance dictionary. That behaviour is the reason why the following code raises an exception:

```
>>> class C:
...     pass
...
>>> c = C()
>>> c.__len__ = lambda: 5
>>> len(c)
Traceback (most recent call last):
  File "<stdin>", line 1, in <module>
TypeError: object of type 'C' has no len()
```

The rationale behind this behaviour lies with a number of special methods such as *__hash__*() and *__repr__*() that are implemented by all objects, including type objects. If the implicit lookup of these methods used the conventional lookup process, they would fail when invoked on the type object itself:

```
>>> 1 .__hash__() == hash(1)
True
>>> int.__hash__() == hash(int)
Traceback (most recent call last):
  File "<stdin>", line 1, in <module>
TypeError: descriptor '__hash__' of 'int' object needs an argument
```

Incorrectly attempting to invoke an unbound method of a class in this way is sometimes referred to as 'metaclass confusion', and is avoided by bypassing the instance when looking up special methods:

```
>>> type(1).__hash__(1) == hash(1)
True
>>> type(int).__hash__(int) == hash(int)
True
```

In addition to bypassing any instance attributes in the interest of correctness, implicit special method lookup generally also bypasses the `__getattribute__()` method even of the object's metaclass:

```
>>> class Meta(type):
...     def __getattribute__(*args):
...         print("Metaclass getattribute invoked")
...         return type.__getattribute__(*args)
...
>>> class C(object, metaclass=Meta):
...     def __len__(self):
...         return 10
...     def __getattribute__(*args):
...         print("Class getattribute invoked")
...         return object.__getattribute__(*args)
...
>>> c = C()
>>> c.__len__()                 # Explicit lookup via instance
Class getattribute invoked
10
>>> type(c).__len__(c)          # Explicit lookup via type
Metaclass getattribute invoked
10
>>> len(c)                      # Implicit lookup
10
```

Bypassing the `__getattribute__()` machinery in this fashion provides significant scope for speed optimisations within the interpreter, at the cost of some flexibility in the handling of special methods (the special method *must* be set on the class object itself in order to be consistently invoked by the interpreter).

3.4 Coroutines

3.4.1 Awaitable Objects

An *awaitable* object generally implements an `__await__()` method. *Coroutine* objects returned from `async def` functions are awaitable.

Note: The *generator iterator* objects returned from generators decorated with `types.coroutine()` or `asyncio.coroutine()` are also awaitable, but they do not implement `__await__()`.

object.**__await__**(*self*)
> Must return an *iterator*. Should be used to implement *awaitable* objects. For instance, `asyncio.Future` implements this method to be compatible with the *await* expression.

New in version 3.5.

See also:

PEP 492 for additional information about awaitable objects.

3.4.2 Coroutine Objects

Coroutine objects are *awaitable* objects. A coroutine's execution can be controlled by calling `__await__()` and iterating over the result. When the coroutine has finished executing and returns, the iterator raises

`StopIteration`, and the exception's `value` attribute holds the return value. If the coroutine raises an exception, it is propagated by the iterator. Coroutines should not directly raise unhandled `StopIteration` exceptions.

Coroutines also have the methods listed below, which are analogous to those of generators (see *Generator-iterator methods*). However, unlike generators, coroutines do not directly support iteration.

Changed in version 3.5.2: It is a `RuntimeError` to await on a coroutine more than once.

`coroutine.send`(*value*)

> Starts or resumes execution of the coroutine. If *value* is `None`, this is equivalent to advancing the iterator returned by *__await__ ()*. If *value* is not `None`, this method delegates to the *send()* method of the iterator that caused the coroutine to suspend. The result (return value, `StopIteration`, or other exception) is the same as when iterating over the *__await__ ()* return value, described above.

`coroutine.throw`(*type*[, *value*[, *traceback*]])

> Raises the specified exception in the coroutine. This method delegates to the *throw()* method of the iterator that caused the coroutine to suspend, if it has such a method. Otherwise, the exception is raised at the suspension point. The result (return value, `StopIteration`, or other exception) is the same as when iterating over the *__await__ ()* return value, described above. If the exception is not caught in the coroutine, it propagates back to the caller.

`coroutine.close`()

> Causes the coroutine to clean itself up and exit. If the coroutine is suspended, this method first delegates to the *close()* method of the iterator that caused the coroutine to suspend, if it has such a method. Then it raises `GeneratorExit` at the suspension point, causing the coroutine to immediately clean itself up. Finally, the coroutine is marked as having finished executing, even if it was never started.
>
> Coroutine objects are automatically closed using the above process when they are about to be destroyed.

3.4.3 Asynchronous Iterators

An *asynchronous iterable* is able to call asynchronous code in its `__aiter__` implementation, and an *asynchronous iterator* can call asynchronous code in its `__anext__` method.

Asynchronous iterators can be used in an *async for* statement.

`object.__aiter__`(*self*)

> Must return an *asynchronous iterator* object.

`object.__anext__`(*self*)

> Must return an *awaitable* resulting in a next value of the iterator. Should raise a `StopAsyncIteration` error when the iteration is over.

An example of an asynchronous iterable object:

```
class Reader:
    async def readline(self):
        ...

    def __aiter__(self):
        return self

    async def __anext__(self):
        val = await self.readline()
        if val == b'':
            raise StopAsyncIteration
        return val
```

New in version 3.5.

> **Note:** Changed in version 3.5.2: Starting with CPython 3.5.2, `__aiter__` can directly return *asynchronous iterators*. Returning an *awaitable* object will result in a `PendingDeprecationWarning`.

The recommended way of writing backwards compatible code in CPython 3.5.x is to continue returning awaitables from `__aiter__`. If you want to avoid the PendingDeprecationWarning and keep the code backwards compatible, the following decorator can be used:

```python
import functools
import sys

if sys.version_info < (3, 5, 2):
    def aiter_compat(func):
        @functools.wraps(func)
        async def wrapper(self):
            return func(self)
        return wrapper
else:
    def aiter_compat(func):
        return func
```

Example:

```python
class AsyncIterator:

    @aiter_compat
    def __aiter__(self):
        return self

    async def __anext__(self):
        ...
```

Starting with CPython 3.6, the `PendingDeprecationWarning` will be replaced with the `DeprecationWarning`. In CPython 3.7, returning an awaitable from `__aiter__` will result in a `RuntimeError`.

3.4.4 Asynchronous Context Managers

An *asynchronous context manager* is a *context manager* that is able to suspend execution in its `__aenter__` and `__aexit__` methods.

Asynchronous context managers can be used in an *async with* statement.

object.`__aenter__`(*self*)
: This method is semantically similar to the *__enter__* (), with only difference that it must return an *awaitable*.

object.`__aexit__`(*self, exc_type, exc_value, traceback*)
: This method is semantically similar to the *__exit__* (), with only difference that it must return an *awaitable*.

An example of an asynchronous context manager class:

```python
class AsyncContextManager:
    async def __aenter__(self):
        await log('entering context')
```

```
async def __aexit__(self, exc_type, exc, tb):
    await log('exiting context')
```

New in version 3.5.

EXECUTION MODEL

4.1 Structure of a program

A Python program is constructed from code blocks. A *block* is a piece of Python program text that is executed as a unit. The following are blocks: a module, a function body, and a class definition. Each command typed interactively is a block. A script file (a file given as standard input to the interpreter or specified as a command line argument to the interpreter) is a code block. A script command (a command specified on the interpreter command line with the '**-c**' option) is a code block. The string argument passed to the built-in functions **eval()** and **exec()** is a code block.

A code block is executed in an *execution frame*. A frame contains some administrative information (used for debugging) and determines where and how execution continues after the code block's execution has completed.

4.2 Naming and binding

4.2.1 Binding of names

Names refer to objects. Names are introduced by name binding operations.

The following constructs bind names: formal parameters to functions, *import* statements, class and function definitions (these bind the class or function name in the defining block), and targets that are identifiers if occurring in an assignment, *for* loop header, or after *as* in a *with* statement or *except* clause. The *import* statement of the form **from ... import *** binds all names defined in the imported module, except those beginning with an underscore. This form may only be used at the module level.

A target occurring in a *del* statement is also considered bound for this purpose (though the actual semantics are to unbind the name).

Each assignment or import statement occurs within a block defined by a class or function definition or at the module level (the top-level code block).

If a name is bound in a block, it is a local variable of that block, unless declared as *nonlocal* or *global*. If a name is bound at the module level, it is a global variable. (The variables of the module code block are local and global.) If a variable is used in a code block but not defined there, it is a *free variable*.

Each occurrence of a name in the program text refers to the *binding* of that name established by the following name resolution rules.

4.2.2 Resolution of names

A *scope* defines the visibility of a name within a block. If a local variable is defined in a block, its scope includes that block. If the definition occurs in a function block, the scope extends to any blocks contained within the defining one, unless a contained block introduces a different binding for the name.

When a name is used in a code block, it is resolved using the nearest enclosing scope. The set of all such scopes visible to a code block is called the block's *environment*.

When a name is not found at all, a `NameError` exception is raised. If the current scope is a function scope, and the name refers to a local variable that has not yet been bound to a value at the point where the name is used, an `UnboundLocalError` exception is raised. `UnboundLocalError` is a subclass of `NameError`.

If a name binding operation occurs anywhere within a code block, all uses of the name within the block are treated as references to the current block. This can lead to errors when a name is used within a block before it is bound. This rule is subtle. Python lacks declarations and allows name binding operations to occur anywhere within a code block. The local variables of a code block can be determined by scanning the entire text of the block for name binding operations.

If the *global* statement occurs within a block, all uses of the name specified in the statement refer to the binding of that name in the top-level namespace. Names are resolved in the top-level namespace by searching the global namespace, i.e. the namespace of the module containing the code block, and the builtins namespace, the namespace of the module `builtins`. The global namespace is searched first. If the name is not found there, the builtins namespace is searched. The *global* statement must precede all uses of the name.

The *global* statement has the same scope as a name binding operation in the same block. If the nearest enclosing scope for a free variable contains a global statement, the free variable is treated as a global.

The *nonlocal* statement causes corresponding names to refer to previously bound variables in the nearest enclosing function scope. `SyntaxError` is raised at compile time if the given name does not exist in any enclosing function scope.

The namespace for a module is automatically created the first time a module is imported. The main module for a script is always called `__main__`.

Class definition blocks and arguments to `exec()` and `eval()` are special in the context of name resolution. A class definition is an executable statement that may use and define names. These references follow the normal rules for name resolution with an exception that unbound local variables are looked up in the global namespace. The namespace of the class definition becomes the attribute dictionary of the class. The scope of names defined in a class block is limited to the class block; it does not extend to the code blocks of methods – this includes comprehensions and generator expressions since they are implemented using a function scope. This means that the following will fail:

```
class A:
    a = 42
    b = list(a + i for i in range(10))
```

4.2.3 Builtins and restricted execution

CPython implementation detail: Users should not touch `__builtins__`; it is strictly an implementation detail. Users wanting to override values in the builtins namespace should *import* the `builtins` module and modify its attributes appropriately.

The builtins namespace associated with the execution of a code block is actually found by looking up the name `__builtins__` in its global namespace; this should be a dictionary or a module (in the latter case the module's dictionary is used). By default, when in the `__main__` module, `__builtins__` is the built-in module `builtins`; when in any other module, `__builtins__` is an alias for the dictionary of the `builtins` module itself.

4.2.4 Interaction with dynamic features

Name resolution of free variables occurs at runtime, not at compile time. This means that the following code will print 42:

```
i = 10
def f():
    print(i)
i = 42
f()
```

The `eval()` and `exec()` functions do not have access to the full environment for resolving names. Names may be resolved in the local and global namespaces of the caller. Free variables are not resolved in the nearest enclosing namespace, but in the global namespace.[1] The `exec()` and `eval()` functions have optional arguments to override the global and local namespace. If only one namespace is specified, it is used for both.

4.3 Exceptions

Exceptions are a means of breaking out of the normal flow of control of a code block in order to handle errors or other exceptional conditions. An exception is *raised* at the point where the error is detected; it may be *handled* by the surrounding code block or by any code block that directly or indirectly invoked the code block where the error occurred.

The Python interpreter raises an exception when it detects a run-time error (such as division by zero). A Python program can also explicitly raise an exception with the *raise* statement. Exception handlers are specified with the *try* … *except* statement. The *finally* clause of such a statement can be used to specify cleanup code which does not handle the exception, but is executed whether an exception occurred or not in the preceding code.

Python uses the "termination" model of error handling: an exception handler can find out what happened and continue execution at an outer level, but it cannot repair the cause of the error and retry the failing operation (except by re-entering the offending piece of code from the top).

When an exception is not handled at all, the interpreter terminates execution of the program, or returns to its interactive main loop. In either case, it prints a stack backtrace, except when the exception is `SystemExit`.

Exceptions are identified by class instances. The *except* clause is selected depending on the class of the instance: it must reference the class of the instance or a base class thereof. The instance can be received by the handler and can carry additional information about the exceptional condition.

Note: Exception messages are not part of the Python API. Their contents may change from one version of Python to the next without warning and should not be relied on by code which will run under multiple versions of the interpreter.

See also the description of the *try* statement in section *The try statement* and *raise* statement in section *The raise statement*.

---

[1] This limitation occurs because the code that is executed by these operations is not available at the time the module is compiled.

THE IMPORT SYSTEM

Python code in one *module* gains access to the code in another module by the process of *importing* it. The *import* statement is the most common way of invoking the import machinery, but it is not the only way. Functions such as `importlib.import_module()` and built-in `__import__()` can also be used to invoke the import machinery.

The *import* statement combines two operations; it searches for the named module, then it binds the results of that search to a name in the local scope. The search operation of the *import* statement is defined as a call to the `__import__()` function, with the appropriate arguments. The return value of `__import__()` is used to perform the name binding operation of the *import* statement. See the *import* statement for the exact details of that name binding operation.

A direct call to `__import__()` performs only the module search and, if found, the module creation operation. While certain side-effects may occur, such as the importing of parent packages, and the updating of various caches (including `sys.modules`), only the *import* statement performs a name binding operation.

When calling `__import__()` as part of an import statement, the standard builtin `__import__()` is called. Other mechanisms for invoking the import system (such as `importlib.import_module()`) may choose to subvert `__import__()` and use its own solution to implement import semantics.

When a module is first imported, Python searches for the module and if found, it creates a module object[1], initializing it. If the named module cannot be found, a `ModuleNotFoundError` is raised. Python implements various strategies to search for the named module when the import machinery is invoked. These strategies can be modified and extended by using various hooks described in the sections below.

Changed in version 3.3: The import system has been updated to fully implement the second phase of PEP 302. There is no longer any implicit import machinery - the full import system is exposed through `sys.meta_path`. In addition, native namespace package support has been implemented (see PEP 420).

5.1 `importlib`

The `importlib` module provides a rich API for interacting with the import system. For example `importlib.import_module()` provides a recommended, simpler API than built-in `__import__()` for invoking the import machinery. Refer to the `importlib` library documentation for additional detail.

5.2 Packages

Python has only one type of module object, and all modules are of this type, regardless of whether the module is implemented in Python, C, or something else. To help organize modules and provide a naming hierarchy, Python has a concept of *packages*.

---

[1] See `types.ModuleType`.

You can think of packages as the directories on a file system and modules as files within directories, but don't take this analogy too literally since packages and modules need not originate from the file system. For the purposes of this documentation, we'll use this convenient analogy of directories and files. Like file system directories, packages are organized hierarchically, and packages may themselves contain subpackages, as well as regular modules.

It's important to keep in mind that all packages are modules, but not all modules are packages. Or put another way, packages are just a special kind of module. Specifically, any module that contains a `__path__` attribute is considered a package.

All modules have a name. Subpackage names are separated from their parent package name by dots, akin to Python's standard attribute access syntax. Thus you might have a module called `sys` and a package called `email`, which in turn has a subpackage called `email.mime` and a module within that subpackage called `email.mime.text`.

5.2.1 Regular packages

Python defines two types of packages, *regular packages* and *namespace packages*. Regular packages are traditional packages as they existed in Python 3.2 and earlier. A regular package is typically implemented as a directory containing an `__init__.py` file. When a regular package is imported, this `__init__.py` file is implicitly executed, and the objects it defines are bound to names in the package's namespace. The `__init__.py` file can contain the same Python code that any other module can contain, and Python will add some additional attributes to the module when it is imported.

For example, the following file system layout defines a top level `parent` package with three subpackages:

```
parent/
    __init__.py
    one/
        __init__.py
    two/
        __init__.py
    three/
        __init__.py
```

Importing `parent.one` will implicitly execute `parent/__init__.py` and `parent/one/__init__.py`. Subsequent imports of `parent.two` or `parent.three` will execute `parent/two/__init__.py` and `parent/three/__init__.py` respectively.

5.2.2 Namespace packages

A namespace package is a composite of various *portions*, where each portion contributes a subpackage to the parent package. Portions may reside in different locations on the file system. Portions may also be found in zip files, on the network, or anywhere else that Python searches during import. Namespace packages may or may not correspond directly to objects on the file system; they may be virtual modules that have no concrete representation.

Namespace packages do not use an ordinary list for their `__path__` attribute. They instead use a custom iterable type which will automatically perform a new search for package portions on the next import attempt within that package if the path of their parent package (or `sys.path` for a top level package) changes.

With namespace packages, there is no `parent/__init__.py` file. In fact, there may be multiple `parent` directories found during import search, where each one is provided by a different portion. Thus `parent/one` may not be physically located next to `parent/two`. In this case, Python will create a namespace package for the top-level `parent` package whenever it or one of its subpackages is imported.

See also PEP 420 for the namespace package specification.

5.3 Searching

To begin the search, Python needs the *fully qualified* name of the module (or package, but for the purposes of this discussion, the difference is immaterial) being imported. This name may come from various arguments to the *import* statement, or from the parameters to the `importlib.import_module()` or `__import__()` functions.

This name will be used in various phases of the import search, and it may be the dotted path to a submodule, e.g. `foo.bar.baz`. In this case, Python first tries to import `foo`, then `foo.bar`, and finally `foo.bar.baz`. If any of the intermediate imports fail, a `ModuleNotFoundError` is raised.

5.3.1 The module cache

The first place checked during import search is `sys.modules`. This mapping serves as a cache of all modules that have been previously imported, including the intermediate paths. So if `foo.bar.baz` was previously imported, `sys.modules` will contain entries for `foo`, `foo.bar`, and `foo.bar.baz`. Each key will have as its value the corresponding module object.

During import, the module name is looked up in `sys.modules` and if present, the associated value is the module satisfying the import, and the process completes. However, if the value is `None`, then a `ModuleNotFoundError` is raised. If the module name is missing, Python will continue searching for the module.

`sys.modules` is writable. Deleting a key may not destroy the associated module (as other modules may hold references to it), but it will invalidate the cache entry for the named module, causing Python to search anew for the named module upon its next import. The key can also be assigned to `None`, forcing the next import of the module to result in a `ModuleNotFoundError`.

Beware though, as if you keep a reference to the module object, invalidate its cache entry in `sys.modules`, and then re-import the named module, the two module objects will *not* be the same. By contrast, `importlib.reload()` will reuse the *same* module object, and simply reinitialise the module contents by rerunning the module's code.

5.3.2 Finders and loaders

If the named module is not found in `sys.modules`, then Python's import protocol is invoked to find and load the module. This protocol consists of two conceptual objects, *finders* and *loaders*. A finder's job is to determine whether it can find the named module using whatever strategy it knows about. Objects that implement both of these interfaces are referred to as *importers* - they return themselves when they find that they can load the requested module.

Python includes a number of default finders and importers. The first one knows how to locate built-in modules, and the second knows how to locate frozen modules. A third default finder searches an *import path* for modules. The *import path* is a list of locations that may name file system paths or zip files. It can also be extended to search for any locatable resource, such as those identified by URLs.

The import machinery is extensible, so new finders can be added to extend the range and scope of module searching.

Finders do not actually load modules. If they can find the named module, they return a *module spec*, an encapsulation of the module's import-related information, which the import machinery then uses when loading the module.

The following sections describe the protocol for finders and loaders in more detail, including how you can create and register new ones to extend the import machinery.

Changed in version 3.4: In previous versions of Python, finders returned *loaders* directly, whereas now they return module specs which *contain* loaders. Loaders are still used during import but have fewer responsibilities.

5.3.3 Import hooks

The import machinery is designed to be extensible; the primary mechanism for this are the *import hooks*. There are two types of import hooks: *meta hooks* and *import path hooks*.

Meta hooks are called at the start of import processing, before any other import processing has occurred, other than `sys.modules` cache look up. This allows meta hooks to override `sys.path` processing, frozen modules, or even built-in modules. Meta hooks are registered by adding new finder objects to `sys.meta_path`, as described below.

Import path hooks are called as part of `sys.path` (or `package.__path__`) processing, at the point where their associated path item is encountered. Import path hooks are registered by adding new callables to `sys.path_hooks` as described below.

5.3.4 The meta path

When the named module is not found in `sys.modules`, Python next searches `sys.meta_path`, which contains a list of meta path finder objects. These finders are queried in order to see if they know how to handle the named module. Meta path finders must implement a method called `find_spec()` which takes three arguments: a name, an import path, and (optionally) a target module. The meta path finder can use any strategy it wants to determine whether it can handle the named module or not.

If the meta path finder knows how to handle the named module, it returns a spec object. If it cannot handle the named module, it returns `None`. If `sys.meta_path` processing reaches the end of its list without returning a spec, then a `ModuleNotFoundError` is raised. Any other exceptions raised are simply propagated up, aborting the import process.

The `find_spec()` method of meta path finders is called with two or three arguments. The first is the fully qualified name of the module being imported, for example `foo.bar.baz`. The second argument is the path entries to use for the module search. For top-level modules, the second argument is `None`, but for submodules or subpackages, the second argument is the value of the parent package's `__path__` attribute. If the appropriate `__path__` attribute cannot be accessed, a `ModuleNotFoundError` is raised. The third argument is an existing module object that will be the target of loading later. The import system passes in a target module only during reload.

The meta path may be traversed multiple times for a single import request. For example, assuming none of the modules involved has already been cached, importing `foo.bar.baz` will first perform a top level import, calling `mpf.find_spec("foo", None, None)` on each meta path finder (`mpf`). After `foo` has been imported, `foo.bar` will be imported by traversing the meta path a second time, calling `mpf.find_spec("foo.bar", foo.__path__, None)`. Once `foo.bar` has been imported, the final traversal will call `mpf.find_spec("foo.bar.baz", foo.bar.__path__, None)`.

Some meta path finders only support top level imports. These importers will always return `None` when anything other than `None` is passed as the second argument.

Python's default `sys.meta_path` has three meta path finders, one that knows how to import built-in modules, one that knows how to import frozen modules, and one that knows how to import modules from an *import path* (i.e. the *path based finder*).

Changed in version 3.4: The `find_spec()` method of meta path finders replaced `find_module()`, which is now deprecated. While it will continue to work without change, the import machinery will try it only if the finder does not implement `find_spec()`.

5.4 Loading

If and when a module spec is found, the import machinery will use it (and the loader it contains) when loading the module. Here is an approximation of what happens during the loading portion of import:

```python
module = None
if spec.loader is not None and hasattr(spec.loader, 'create_module'):
    # It is assumed 'exec_module' will also be defined on the loader.
    module = spec.loader.create_module(spec)
if module is None:
    module = ModuleType(spec.name)
# The import-related module attributes get set here:
_init_module_attrs(spec, module)

if spec.loader is None:
    if spec.submodule_search_locations is not None:
        # namespace package
        sys.modules[spec.name] = module
    else:
        # unsupported
        raise ImportError
elif not hasattr(spec.loader, 'exec_module'):
    module = spec.loader.load_module(spec.name)
    # Set __loader__ and __package__ if missing.
else:
    sys.modules[spec.name] = module
    try:
        spec.loader.exec_module(module)
    except BaseException:
        try:
            del sys.modules[spec.name]
        except KeyError:
            pass
        raise
return sys.modules[spec.name]
```

Note the following details:

- If there is an existing module object with the given name in `sys.modules`, import will have already returned it.

- The module will exist in `sys.modules` before the loader executes the module code. This is crucial because the module code may (directly or indirectly) import itself; adding it to `sys.modules` beforehand prevents unbounded recursion in the worst case and multiple loading in the best.

- If loading fails, the failing module – and only the failing module – gets removed from `sys.modules`. Any module already in the `sys.modules` cache, and any module that was successfully loaded as a side-effect, must remain in the cache. This contrasts with reloading where even the failing module is left in `sys.modules`.

- After the module is created but before execution, the import machinery sets the import-related module attributes ("_init_module_attrs" in the pseudo-code example above), as summarized in a *later section*.

- Module execution is the key moment of loading in which the module's namespace gets populated. Execution is entirely delegated to the loader, which gets to decide what gets populated and how.

- The module created during loading and passed to exec_module() may not be the one returned at the end of import[2].

---

[2] The importlib implementation avoids using the return value directly. Instead, it gets the module object by looking the

Changed in version 3.4: The import system has taken over the boilerplate responsibilities of loaders. These were previously performed by the `importlib.abc.Loader.load_module()` method.

5.4.1 Loaders

Module loaders provide the critical function of loading: module execution. The import machinery calls the `importlib.abc.Loader.exec_module()` method with a single argument, the module object to execute. Any value returned from `exec_module()` is ignored.

Loaders must satisfy the following requirements:

- If the module is a Python module (as opposed to a built-in module or a dynamically loaded extension), the loader should execute the module's code in the module's global name space (`module.__dict__`).

- If the loader cannot execute the module, it should raise an `ImportError`, although any other exception raised during `exec_module()` will be propagated.

In many cases, the finder and loader can be the same object; in such cases the `find_spec()` method would just return a spec with the loader set to `self`.

Module loaders may opt in to creating the module object during loading by implementing a `create_module()` method. It takes one argument, the module spec, and returns the new module object to use during loading. `create_module()` does not need to set any attributes on the module object. If the method returns `None`, the import machinery will create the new module itself.

New in version 3.4: The `create_module()` method of loaders.

Changed in version 3.4: The `load_module()` method was replaced by `exec_module()` and the import machinery assumed all the boilerplate responsibilities of loading.

For compatibility with existing loaders, the import machinery will use the `load_module()` method of loaders if it exists and the loader does not also implement `exec_module()`. However, `load_module()` has been deprecated and loaders should implement `exec_module()` instead.

The `load_module()` method must implement all the boilerplate loading functionality described above in addition to executing the module. All the same constraints apply, with some additional clarification:

- If there is an existing module object with the given name in `sys.modules`, the loader must use that existing module. (Otherwise, `importlib.reload()` will not work correctly.) If the named module does not exist in `sys.modules`, the loader must create a new module object and add it to `sys.modules`.

- The module *must* exist in `sys.modules` before the loader executes the module code, to prevent unbounded recursion or multiple loading.

- If loading fails, the loader must remove any modules it has inserted into `sys.modules`, but it must remove **only** the failing module(s), and only if the loader itself has loaded the module(s) explicitly.

Changed in version 3.5: A `DeprecationWarning` is raised when `exec_module()` is defined but `create_module()` is not.

Changed in version 3.6: An `ImportError` is raised when `exec_module()` is defined but `create_module()` is not.

5.4.2 Submodules

When a submodule is loaded using any mechanism (e.g. `importlib` APIs, the `import` or `import-from` statements, or built-in `__import__()`) a binding is placed in the parent module's namespace to the submodule

---

module name up in `sys.modules`. The indirect effect of this is that an imported module may replace itself in `sys.modules`. This is implementation-specific behavior that is not guaranteed to work in other Python implementations.

object. For example, if package `spam` has a submodule `foo`, after importing `spam.foo`, `spam` will have an attribute `foo` which is bound to the submodule. Let's say you have the following directory structure:

```
spam/
    __init__.py
    foo.py
    bar.py
```

and `spam/__init__.py` has the following lines in it:

```
from .foo import Foo
from .bar import Bar
```

then executing the following puts a name binding to `foo` and `bar` in the `spam` module:

```
>>> import spam
>>> spam.foo
<module 'spam.foo' from '/tmp/imports/spam/foo.py'>
>>> spam.bar
<module 'spam.bar' from '/tmp/imports/spam/bar.py'>
```

Given Python's familiar name binding rules this might seem surprising, but it's actually a fundamental feature of the import system. The invariant holding is that if you have `sys.modules['spam']` and `sys.modules['spam.foo']` (as you would after the above import), the latter must appear as the `foo` attribute of the former.

5.4.3 Module spec

The import machinery uses a variety of information about each module during import, especially before loading. Most of the information is common to all modules. The purpose of a module's spec is to encapsulate this import-related information on a per-module basis.

Using a spec during import allows state to be transferred between import system components, e.g. between the finder that creates the module spec and the loader that executes it. Most importantly, it allows the import machinery to perform the boilerplate operations of loading, whereas without a module spec the loader had that responsibility.

The module's spec is exposed as the `__spec__` attribute on a module object. See `ModuleSpec` for details on the contents of the module spec.

New in version 3.4.

5.4.4 Import-related module attributes

The import machinery fills in these attributes on each module object during loading, based on the module's spec, before the loader executes the module.

`__name__`
> The `__name__` attribute must be set to the fully-qualified name of the module. This name is used to uniquely identify the module in the import system.

`__loader__`
> The `__loader__` attribute must be set to the loader object that the import machinery used when loading the module. This is mostly for introspection, but can be used for additional loader-specific functionality, for example getting data associated with a loader.

__package__

> The module's `__package__` attribute must be set. Its value must be a string, but it can be the same value as its `__name__`. When the module is a package, its `__package__` value should be set to its `__name__`. When the module is not a package, `__package__` should be set to the empty string for top-level modules, or for submodules, to the parent package's name. See PEP 366 for further details.
>
> This attribute is used instead of `__name__` to calculate explicit relative imports for main modules, as defined in PEP 366. It is expected to have the same value as `__spec__.parent`.
>
> Changed in version 3.6: The value of `__package__` is expected to be the same as `__spec__.parent`.

__spec__

> The `__spec__` attribute must be set to the module spec that was used when importing the module. Setting `__spec__` appropriately applies equally to *modules initialized during interpreter startup*. The one exception is `__main__`, where `__spec__` is *set to None in some cases*.
>
> When `__package__` is not defined, `__spec__.parent` is used as a fallback.
>
> New in version 3.4.
>
> Changed in version 3.6: `__spec__.parent` is used as a fallback when `__package__` is not defined.

__path__

> If the module is a package (either regular or namespace), the module object's `__path__` attribute must be set. The value must be iterable, but may be empty if `__path__` has no further significance. If `__path__` is not empty, it must produce strings when iterated over. More details on the semantics of `__path__` are given *below*.
>
> Non-package modules should not have a `__path__` attribute.

__file__

__cached__

> `__file__` is optional. If set, this attribute's value must be a string. The import system may opt to leave `__file__` unset if it has no semantic meaning (e.g. a module loaded from a database).
>
> If `__file__` is set, it may also be appropriate to set the `__cached__` attribute which is the path to any compiled version of the code (e.g. byte-compiled file). The file does not need to exist to set this attribute; the path can simply point to where the compiled file would exist (see PEP 3147).
>
> It is also appropriate to set `__cached__` when `__file__` is not set. However, that scenario is quite atypical. Ultimately, the loader is what makes use of `__file__` and/or `__cached__`. So if a loader can load from a cached module but otherwise does not load from a file, that atypical scenario may be appropriate.

5.4.5 module.__path__

By definition, if a module has a `__path__` attribute, it is a package, regardless of its value.

A package's `__path__` attribute is used during imports of its subpackages. Within the import machinery, it functions much the same as `sys.path`, i.e. providing a list of locations to search for modules during import. However, `__path__` is typically much more constrained than `sys.path`.

`__path__` must be an iterable of strings, but it may be empty. The same rules used for `sys.path` also apply to a package's `__path__`, and `sys.path_hooks` (described below) are consulted when traversing a package's `__path__`.

A package's `__init__.py` file may set or alter the package's `__path__` attribute, and this was typically the way namespace packages were implemented prior to PEP 420. With the adoption of PEP 420, namespace packages no longer need to supply `__init__.py` files containing only `__path__` manipulation code; the import machinery automatically sets `__path__` correctly for the namespace package.

5.4.6 Module reprs

By default, all modules have a usable repr, however depending on the attributes set above, and in the module's spec, you can more explicitly control the repr of module objects.

If the module has a spec (`__spec__`), the import machinery will try to generate a repr from it. If that fails or there is no spec, the import system will craft a default repr using whatever information is available on the module. It will try to use the `module.__name__`, `module.__file__`, and `module.__loader__` as input into the repr, with defaults for whatever information is missing.

Here are the exact rules used:

- If the module has a `__spec__` attribute, the information in the spec is used to generate the repr. The "name", "loader", "origin", and "has_location" attributes are consulted.

- If the module has a `__file__` attribute, this is used as part of the module's repr.

- If the module has no `__file__` but does have a `__loader__` that is not `None`, then the loader's repr is used as part of the module's repr.

- Otherwise, just use the module's `__name__` in the repr.

Changed in version 3.4: Use of `loader.module_repr()` has been deprecated and the module spec is now used by the import machinery to generate a module repr.

For backward compatibility with Python 3.3, the module repr will be generated by calling the loader's `module_repr()` method, if defined, before trying either approach described above. However, the method is deprecated.

5.5 The Path Based Finder

As mentioned previously, Python comes with several default meta path finders. One of these, called the *path based finder* (`PathFinder`), searches an *import path*, which contains a list of *path entries*. Each path entry names a location to search for modules.

The path based finder itself doesn't know how to import anything. Instead, it traverses the individual path entries, associating each of them with a path entry finder that knows how to handle that particular kind of path.

The default set of path entry finders implement all the semantics for finding modules on the file system, handling special file types such as Python source code (`.py` files), Python byte code (`.pyc` files) and shared libraries (e.g. `.so` files). When supported by the `zipimport` module in the standard library, the default path entry finders also handle loading all of these file types (other than shared libraries) from zipfiles.

Path entries need not be limited to file system locations. They can refer to URLs, database queries, or any other location that can be specified as a string.

The path based finder provides additional hooks and protocols so that you can extend and customize the types of searchable path entries. For example, if you wanted to support path entries as network URLs, you could write a hook that implements HTTP semantics to find modules on the web. This hook (a callable) would return a *path entry finder* supporting the protocol described below, which was then used to get a loader for the module from the web.

A word of warning: this section and the previous both use the term *finder*, distinguishing between them by using the terms *meta path finder* and *path entry finder*. These two types of finders are very similar, support similar protocols, and function in similar ways during the import process, but it's important to keep in mind that they are subtly different. In particular, meta path finders operate at the beginning of the import process, as keyed off the `sys.meta_path` traversal.

By contrast, path entry finders are in a sense an implementation detail of the path based finder, and in fact, if the path based finder were to be removed from `sys.meta_path`, none of the path entry finder semantics would be invoked.

5.5.1 Path entry finders

The *path based finder* is responsible for finding and loading Python modules and packages whose location is specified with a string *path entry*. Most path entries name locations in the file system, but they need not be limited to this.

As a meta path finder, the *path based finder* implements the `find_spec()` protocol previously described, however it exposes additional hooks that can be used to customize how modules are found and loaded from the *import path*.

Three variables are used by the *path based finder*, `sys.path`, `sys.path_hooks` and `sys.path_importer_cache`. The `__path__` attributes on package objects are also used. These provide additional ways that the import machinery can be customized.

`sys.path` contains a list of strings providing search locations for modules and packages. It is initialized from the `PYTHONPATH` environment variable and various other installation- and implementation-specific defaults. Entries in `sys.path` can name directories on the file system, zip files, and potentially other "locations" (see the `site` module) that should be searched for modules, such as URLs, or database queries. Only strings and bytes should be present on `sys.path`; all other data types are ignored. The encoding of bytes entries is determined by the individual *path entry finders*.

The *path based finder* is a *meta path finder*, so the import machinery begins the *import path* search by calling the path based finder's `find_spec()` method as described previously. When the `path` argument to `find_spec()` is given, it will be a list of string paths to traverse - typically a package's `__path__` attribute for an import within that package. If the `path` argument is `None`, this indicates a top level import and `sys.path` is used.

The path based finder iterates over every entry in the search path, and for each of these, looks for an appropriate *path entry finder* (`PathEntryFinder`) for the path entry. Because this can be an expensive operation (e.g. there may be *stat()* call overheads for this search), the path based finder maintains a cache mapping path entries to path entry finders. This cache is maintained in `sys.path_importer_cache` (despite the name, this cache actually stores finder objects rather than being limited to *importer* objects). In this way, the expensive search for a particular *path entry* location's *path entry finder* need only be done once. User code is free to remove cache entries from `sys.path_importer_cache` forcing the path based finder to perform the path entry search again[3].

If the path entry is not present in the cache, the path based finder iterates over every callable in `sys.path_hooks`. Each of the *path entry hooks* in this list is called with a single argument, the path entry to be searched. This callable may either return a *path entry finder* that can handle the path entry, or it may raise `ImportError`. An `ImportError` is used by the path based finder to signal that the hook cannot find a *path entry finder* for that *path entry*. The exception is ignored and *import path* iteration continues. The hook should expect either a string or bytes object; the encoding of bytes objects is up to the hook (e.g. it may be a file system encoding, UTF-8, or something else), and if the hook cannot decode the argument, it should raise `ImportError`.

If `sys.path_hooks` iteration ends with no *path entry finder* being returned, then the path based finder's `find_spec()` method will store `None` in `sys.path_importer_cache` (to indicate that there is no finder for this path entry) and return `None`, indicating that this *meta path finder* could not find the module.

If a *path entry finder* *is* returned by one of the *path entry hook* callables on `sys.path_hooks`, then the following protocol is used to ask the finder for a module spec, which is then used when loading the module.

---

[3] In legacy code, it is possible to find instances of `imp.NullImporter` in the `sys.path_importer_cache`. It is recommended that code be changed to use `None` instead. See portingpythoncode for more details.

The current working directory – denoted by an empty string – is handled slightly differently from other entries on `sys.path`. First, if the current working directory is found to not exist, no value is stored in `sys.path_importer_cache`. Second, the value for the current working directory is looked up fresh for each module lookup. Third, the path used for `sys.path_importer_cache` and returned by `importlib.machinery.PathFinder.find_spec()` will be the actual current working directory and not the empty string.

5.5.2 Path entry finder protocol

In order to support imports of modules and initialized packages and also to contribute portions to namespace packages, path entry finders must implement the `find_spec()` method.

`find_spec()` takes two argument, the fully qualified name of the module being imported, and the (optional) target module. `find_spec()` returns a fully populated spec for the module. This spec will always have "loader" set (with one exception).

To indicate to the import machinery that the spec represents a namespace *portion*. the path entry finder sets "loader" on the spec to `None` and "submodule_search_locations" to a list containing the portion.

Changed in version 3.4: `find_spec()` replaced `find_loader()` and `find_module()`, both of which are now deprecated, but will be used if `find_spec()` is not defined.

Older path entry finders may implement one of these two deprecated methods instead of `find_spec()`. The methods are still respected for the sake of backward compatibility. However, if `find_spec()` is implemented on the path entry finder, the legacy methods are ignored.

`find_loader()` takes one argument, the fully qualified name of the module being imported. `find_loader()` returns a 2-tuple where the first item is the loader and the second item is a namespace *portion*. When the first item (i.e. the loader) is `None`, this means that while the path entry finder does not have a loader for the named module, it knows that the path entry contributes to a namespace portion for the named module. This will almost always be the case where Python is asked to import a namespace package that has no physical presence on the file system. When a path entry finder returns `None` for the loader, the second item of the 2-tuple return value must be a sequence, although it can be empty.

If `find_loader()` returns a non-`None` loader value, the portion is ignored and the loader is returned from the path based finder, terminating the search through the path entries.

For backwards compatibility with other implementations of the import protocol, many path entry finders also support the same, traditional `find_module()` method that meta path finders support. However path entry finder `find_module()` methods are never called with a `path` argument (they are expected to record the appropriate path information from the initial call to the path hook).

The `find_module()` method on path entry finders is deprecated, as it does not allow the path entry finder to contribute portions to namespace packages. If both `find_loader()` and `find_module()` exist on a path entry finder, the import system will always call `find_loader()` in preference to `find_module()`.

5.6 Replacing the standard import system

The most reliable mechanism for replacing the entire import system is to delete the default contents of `sys.meta_path`, replacing them entirely with a custom meta path hook.

If it is acceptable to only alter the behaviour of import statements without affecting other APIs that access the import system, then replacing the builtin `__import__()` function may be sufficient. This technique may also be employed at the module level to only alter the behaviour of import statements within that module.

To selectively prevent import of some modules from a hook early on the meta path (rather than disabling the standard import system entirely), it is sufficient to raise `ModuleNotFoundError` directly from `find_spec()` instead of returning `None`. The latter indicates that the meta path search should continue, while raising an exception terminates it immediately.

5.7 Special considerations for __main__

The `__main__` module is a special case relative to Python's import system. As noted *elsewhere*, the `__main__` module is directly initialized at interpreter startup, much like `sys` and `builtins`. However, unlike those two, it doesn't strictly qualify as a built-in module. This is because the manner in which `__main__` is initialized depends on the flags and other options with which the interpreter is invoked.

5.7.1 __main__.__spec__

Depending on how `__main__` is initialized, `__main__.__spec__` gets set appropriately or to `None`.

When Python is started with the -m option, `__spec__` is set to the module spec of the corresponding module or package. `__spec__` is also populated when the `__main__` module is loaded as part of executing a directory, zipfile or other `sys.path` entry.

In the remaining cases `__main__.__spec__` is set to `None`, as the code used to populate the `__main__` does not correspond directly with an importable module:

- interactive prompt
- -c switch
- running from stdin
- running directly from a source or bytecode file

Note that `__main__.__spec__` is always `None` in the last case, *even if* the file could technically be imported directly as a module instead. Use the -m switch if valid module metadata is desired in `__main__`.

Note also that even when `__main__` corresponds with an importable module and `__main__.__spec__` is set accordingly, they're still considered *distinct* modules. This is due to the fact that blocks guarded by `if __name__ == "__main__":` checks only execute when the module is used to populate the `__main__` namespace, and not during normal import.

5.8 Open issues

XXX It would be really nice to have a diagram.

XXX * (import_machinery.rst) how about a section devoted just to the attributes of modules and packages, perhaps expanding upon or supplanting the related entries in the data model reference page?

XXX runpy, pkgutil, et al in the library manual should all get "See Also" links at the top pointing to the new import system section.

XXX Add more explanation regarding the different ways in which `__main__` is initialized?

XXX Add more info on `__main__` quirks/pitfalls (i.e. copy from PEP 395).

5.9 References

The import machinery has evolved considerably since Python's early days. The original specification for packages is still available to read, although some details have changed since the writing of that document.

The original specification for `sys.meta_path` was PEP 302, with subsequent extension in PEP 420.

PEP 420 introduced *namespace packages* for Python 3.3. PEP 420 also introduced the `find_loader()` protocol as an alternative to `find_module()`.

PEP 366 describes the addition of the `__package__` attribute for explicit relative imports in main modules.

PEP 328 introduced absolute and explicit relative imports and initially proposed `__name__` for semantics PEP 366 would eventually specify for `__package__`.

PEP 338 defines executing modules as scripts.

PEP 451 adds the encapsulation of per-module import state in spec objects. It also off-loads most of the boilerplate responsibilities of loaders back onto the import machinery. These changes allow the deprecation of several APIs in the import system and also addition of new methods to finders and loaders.

EXPRESSIONS

This chapter explains the meaning of the elements of expressions in Python.

Syntax Notes: In this and the following chapters, extended BNF notation will be used to describe syntax, not lexical analysis. When (one alternative of) a syntax rule has the form

```
name    ::=    othername
```

and no semantics are given, the semantics of this form of **name** are the same as for **othername**.

6.1 Arithmetic conversions

When a description of an arithmetic operator below uses the phrase "the numeric arguments are converted to a common type," this means that the operator implementation for built-in types works as follows:

- If either argument is a complex number, the other is converted to complex;
- otherwise, if either argument is a floating point number, the other is converted to floating point;
- otherwise, both must be integers and no conversion is necessary.

Some additional rules apply for certain operators (e.g., a string as a left argument to the '%' operator). Extensions must define their own conversion behavior.

6.2 Atoms

Atoms are the most basic elements of expressions. The simplest atoms are identifiers or literals. Forms enclosed in parentheses, brackets or braces are also categorized syntactically as atoms. The syntax for atoms is:

```
atom        ::=    identifier | literal | enclosure
enclosure   ::=    parenth_form | list_display | dict_display | set_display
                   | generator_expression | yield_atom
```

6.2.1 Identifiers (Names)

An identifier occurring as an atom is a name. See section *Identifiers and keywords* for lexical definition and section *Naming and binding* for documentation of naming and binding.

When the name is bound to an object, evaluation of the atom yields that object. When a name is not bound, an attempt to evaluate it raises a `NameError` exception.

Private name mangling: When an identifier that textually occurs in a class definition begins with two or more underscore characters and does not end in two or more underscores, it is considered a *private name* of that class. Private names are transformed to a longer form before code is generated for them. The transformation inserts the class name, with leading underscores removed and a single underscore inserted, in front of the name. For example, the identifier `__spam` occurring in a class named `Ham` will be transformed to `_Ham__spam`. This transformation is independent of the syntactical context in which the identifier is used. If the transformed name is extremely long (longer than 255 characters), implementation defined truncation may happen. If the class name consists only of underscores, no transformation is done.

6.2.2 Literals

Python supports string and bytes literals and various numeric literals:

```
literal    ::=    stringliteral | bytesliteral
                  | integer | floatnumber | imagnumber
```

Evaluation of a literal yields an object of the given type (string, bytes, integer, floating point number, complex number) with the given value. The value may be approximated in the case of floating point and imaginary (complex) literals. See section *Literals* for details.

All literals correspond to immutable data types, and hence the object's identity is less important than its value. Multiple evaluations of literals with the same value (either the same occurrence in the program text or a different occurrence) may obtain the same object or a different object with the same value.

6.2.3 Parenthesized forms

A parenthesized form is an optional expression list enclosed in parentheses:

```
parenth_form   ::=    "(" [starred_expression] ")"
```

A parenthesized expression list yields whatever that expression list yields: if the list contains at least one comma, it yields a tuple; otherwise, it yields the single expression that makes up the expression list.

An empty pair of parentheses yields an empty tuple object. Since tuples are immutable, the rules for literals apply (i.e., two occurrences of the empty tuple may or may not yield the same object).

Note that tuples are not formed by the parentheses, but rather by use of the comma operator. The exception is the empty tuple, for which parentheses *are* required — allowing unparenthesized "nothing" in expressions would cause ambiguities and allow common typos to pass uncaught.

6.2.4 Displays for lists, sets and dictionaries

For constructing a list, a set or a dictionary Python provides special syntax called "displays", each of them in two flavors:

- either the container contents are listed explicitly, or
- they are computed via a set of looping and filtering instructions, called a *comprehension*.

Common syntax elements for comprehensions are:

```
comprehension   ::=   expression comp_for
comp_for        ::=   [ASYNC] "for" target_list "in" or_test [comp_iter]
comp_iter       ::=   comp_for | comp_if
comp_if         ::=   "if" expression_nocond [comp_iter]
```

The comprehension consists of a single expression followed by at least one *for* clause and zero or more *for* or *if* clauses. In this case, the elements of the new container are those that would be produced by considering each of the *for* or *if* clauses a block, nesting from left to right, and evaluating the expression to produce an element each time the innermost block is reached.

Note that the comprehension is executed in a separate scope, so names assigned to in the target list don't "leak" into the enclosing scope.

Since Python 3.6, in an *async def* function, an *async for* clause may be used to iterate over a *asynchronous iterator*. A comprehension in an *async def* function may consist of either a *for* or *async for* clause following the leading expression, may contain additional *for* or *async for* clauses, and may also use *await* expressions. If a comprehension contains either *async for* clauses or *await* expressions it is called an *asynchronous comprehension*. An asynchronous comprehension may suspend the execution of the coroutine function in which it appears. See also PEP 530.

6.2.5 List displays

A list display is a possibly empty series of expressions enclosed in square brackets:

```
list_display   ::=   "[" [starred_list | comprehension] "]"
```

A list display yields a new list object, the contents being specified by either a list of expressions or a comprehension. When a comma-separated list of expressions is supplied, its elements are evaluated from left to right and placed into the list object in that order. When a comprehension is supplied, the list is constructed from the elements resulting from the comprehension.

6.2.6 Set displays

A set display is denoted by curly braces and distinguishable from dictionary displays by the lack of colons separating keys and values:

```
set_display   ::=   "{" (starred_list | comprehension) "}"
```

A set display yields a new mutable set object, the contents being specified by either a sequence of expressions or a comprehension. When a comma-separated list of expressions is supplied, its elements are evaluated from left to right and added to the set object. When a comprehension is supplied, the set is constructed from the elements resulting from the comprehension.

An empty set cannot be constructed with {}; this literal constructs an empty dictionary.

6.2.7 Dictionary displays

A dictionary display is a possibly empty series of key/datum pairs enclosed in curly braces:

```
dict_display       ::=   "{" [key_datum_list | dict_comprehension] "}"
key_datum_list     ::=   key_datum ("," key_datum)* [","]
```

```
key_datum          ::=  expression ":" expression | "**" or_expr
dict_comprehension ::=  expression ":" expression comp_for
```

A dictionary display yields a new dictionary object.

If a comma-separated sequence of key/datum pairs is given, they are evaluated from left to right to define the entries of the dictionary: each key object is used as a key into the dictionary to store the corresponding datum. This means that you can specify the same key multiple times in the key/datum list, and the final dictionary's value for that key will be the last one given.

A double asterisk ** denotes *dictionary unpacking*. Its operand must be a *mapping*. Each mapping item is added to the new dictionary. Later values replace values already set by earlier key/datum pairs and earlier dictionary unpackings.

New in version 3.5: Unpacking into dictionary displays, originally proposed by PEP 448.

A dict comprehension, in contrast to list and set comprehensions, needs two expressions separated with a colon followed by the usual "for" and "if" clauses. When the comprehension is run, the resulting key and value elements are inserted in the new dictionary in the order they are produced.

Restrictions on the types of the key values are listed earlier in section *The standard type hierarchy*. (To summarize, the key type should be *hashable*, which excludes all mutable objects.) Clashes between duplicate keys are not detected; the last datum (textually rightmost in the display) stored for a given key value prevails.

6.2.8 Generator expressions

A generator expression is a compact generator notation in parentheses:

```
generator_expression ::=  "(" expression comp_for ")"
```

A generator expression yields a new generator object. Its syntax is the same as for comprehensions, except that it is enclosed in parentheses instead of brackets or curly braces.

Variables used in the generator expression are evaluated lazily when the `__next__()` method is called for the generator object (in the same fashion as normal generators). However, the leftmost *for* clause is immediately evaluated, so that an error produced by it can be seen before any other possible error in the code that handles the generator expression. Subsequent *for* clauses cannot be evaluated immediately since they may depend on the previous *for* loop. For example: `(x*y for x in range(10) for y in bar(x))`.

The parentheses can be omitted on calls with only one argument. See section *Calls* for details.

Since Python 3.6, if the generator appears in an *async def* function, then *async for* clauses and *await* expressions are permitted as with an asynchronous comprehension. If a generator expression contains either *async for* clauses or *await* expressions it is called an *asynchronous generator expression*. An asynchronous generator expression yields a new asynchronous generator object, which is an asynchronous iterator (see *Asynchronous Iterators*).

6.2.9 Yield expressions

```
yield_atom        ::=  "(" yield_expression ")"
yield_expression  ::=  "yield" [expression_list | "from" expression]
```

The yield expression is used when defining a *generator* function or an *asynchronous generator* function and thus can only be used in the body of a function definition. Using a yield expression in a function's body causes that function to be a generator, and using it in an *async def* function's body causes that coroutine function to be an asynchronous generator. For example:

```
def gen():  # defines a generator function
    yield 123

async def agen():  # defines an asynchronous generator function (PEP 525)
    yield 123
```

Generator functions are described below, while asynchronous generator functions are described separately in section *Asynchronous generator functions*.

When a generator function is called, it returns an iterator known as a generator. That generator then controls the execution of the generator function. The execution starts when one of the generator's methods is called. At that time, the execution proceeds to the first yield expression, where it is suspended again, returning the value of *expression_list* to the generator's caller. By suspended, we mean that all local state is retained, including the current bindings of local variables, the instruction pointer, the internal evaluation stack, and the state of any exception handling. When the execution is resumed by calling one of the generator's methods, the function can proceed exactly as if the yield expression were just another external call. The value of the yield expression after resuming depends on the method which resumed the execution. If `__next__()` is used (typically via either a *for* or the `next()` builtin) then the result is None. Otherwise, if *send()* is used, then the result will be the value passed in to that method.

All of this makes generator functions quite similar to coroutines; they yield multiple times, they have more than one entry point and their execution can be suspended. The only difference is that a generator function cannot control where the execution should continue after it yields; the control is always transferred to the generator's caller.

Yield expressions are allowed anywhere in a *try* construct. If the generator is not resumed before it is finalized (by reaching a zero reference count or by being garbage collected), the generator-iterator's *close()* method will be called, allowing any pending *finally* clauses to execute.

When `yield from <expr>` is used, it treats the supplied expression as a subiterator. All values produced by that subiterator are passed directly to the caller of the current generator's methods. Any values passed in with *send()* and any exceptions passed in with *throw()* are passed to the underlying iterator if it has the appropriate methods. If this is not the case, then *send()* will raise AttributeError or TypeError, while *throw()* will just raise the passed in exception immediately.

When the underlying iterator is complete, the `value` attribute of the raised StopIteration instance becomes the value of the yield expression. It can be either set explicitly when raising StopIteration, or automatically when the sub-iterator is a generator (by returning a value from the sub-generator).

Changed in version 3.3: Added `yield from <expr>` to delegate control flow to a subiterator.

The parentheses may be omitted when the yield expression is the sole expression on the right hand side of an assignment statement.

See also:

PEP 255 - **Simple Generators** The proposal for adding generators and the *yield* statement to Python.

PEP 342 - **Coroutines via Enhanced Generators** The proposal to enhance the API and syntax of generators, making them usable as simple coroutines.

PEP 380 - **Syntax for Delegating to a Subgenerator** The proposal to introduce the `yield_from` syntax, making delegation to sub-generators easy.

Generator-iterator methods

This subsection describes the methods of a generator iterator. They can be used to control the execution of a generator function.

Note that calling any of the generator methods below when the generator is already executing raises a `ValueError` exception.

generator.__next__()

Starts the execution of a generator function or resumes it at the last executed yield expression. When a generator function is resumed with a *__next__* () method, the current yield expression always evaluates to `None`. The execution then continues to the next yield expression, where the generator is suspended again, and the value of the *expression_list* is returned to *__next__* ()'s caller. If the generator exits without yielding another value, a `StopIteration` exception is raised.

This method is normally called implicitly, e.g. by a *for* loop, or by the built-in `next()` function.

generator.send(*value*)

Resumes the execution and "sends" a value into the generator function. The *value* argument becomes the result of the current yield expression. The *send()* method returns the next value yielded by the generator, or raises `StopIteration` if the generator exits without yielding another value. When *send()* is called to start the generator, it must be called with `None` as the argument, because there is no yield expression that could receive the value.

generator.throw(*type*[, *value*[, *traceback*]])

Raises an exception of type `type` at the point where the generator was paused, and returns the next value yielded by the generator function. If the generator exits without yielding another value, a `StopIteration` exception is raised. If the generator function does not catch the passed-in exception, or raises a different exception, then that exception propagates to the caller.

generator.close()

Raises a `GeneratorExit` at the point where the generator function was paused. If the generator function then exits gracefully, is already closed, or raises `GeneratorExit` (by not catching the exception), close returns to its caller. If the generator yields a value, a `RuntimeError` is raised. If the generator raises any other exception, it is propagated to the caller. *close()* does nothing if the generator has already exited due to an exception or normal exit.

Examples

Here is a simple example that demonstrates the behavior of generators and generator functions:

```
>>> def echo(value=None):
...     print("Execution starts when 'next()' is called for the first time.")
...     try:
...         while True:
...             try:
...                 value = (yield value)
...             except Exception as e:
...                 value = e
...     finally:
...         print("Don't forget to clean up when 'close()' is called.")
...
>>> generator = echo(1)
>>> print(next(generator))
Execution starts when 'next()' is called for the first time.
1
>>> print(next(generator))
None
>>> print(generator.send(2))
2
>>> generator.throw(TypeError, "spam")
TypeError('spam',)
```

```
>>> generator.close()
Don't forget to clean up when 'close()' is called.
```

For examples using `yield from`, see pep-380 in "What's New in Python."

Asynchronous generator functions

The presence of a yield expression in a function or method defined using *async def* further defines the function as a *asynchronous generator* function.

When an asynchronous generator function is called, it returns an asynchronous iterator known as an asynchronous generator object. That object then controls the execution of the generator function. An asynchronous generator object is typically used in an *async for* statement in a coroutine function analogously to how a generator object would be used in a *for* statement.

Calling one of the asynchronous generator's methods returns an *awaitable* object, and the execution starts when this object is awaited on. At that time, the execution proceeds to the first yield expression, where it is suspended again, returning the value of *expression_list* to the awaiting coroutine. As with a generator, suspension means that all local state is retained, including the current bindings of local variables, the instruction pointer, the internal evaluation stack, and the state of any exception handling. When the execution is resumed by awaiting on the next object returned by the asynchronous generator's methods, the function can proceed exactly as if the yield expression were just another external call. The value of the yield expression after resuming depends on the method which resumed the execution. If *__anext__ ()* is used then the result is **None**. Otherwise, if *asend()* is used, then the result will be the value passed in to that method.

In an asynchronous generator function, yield expressions are allowed anywhere in a *try* construct. However, if an asynchronous generator is not resumed before it is finalized (by reaching a zero reference count or by being garbage collected), then a yield expression within a *try* construct could result in a failure to execute pending *finally* clauses. In this case, it is the responsibility of the event loop or scheduler running the asynchronous generator to call the asynchronous generator-iterator's *aclose()* method and run the resulting coroutine object, thus allowing any pending *finally* clauses to execute.

To take care of finalization, an event loop should define a *finalizer* function which takes an asynchronous generator-iterator and presumably calls *aclose()* and executes the coroutine. This *finalizer* may be registered by calling `sys.set_asyncgen_hooks()`. When first iterated over, an asynchronous generator-iterator will store the registered *finalizer* to be called upon finalization. For a reference example of a *finalizer* method see the implementation of `asyncio.Loop.shutdown_asyncgens` in Lib/asyncio/base_events.py.

The expression `yield from <expr>` is a syntax error when used in an asynchronous generator function.

Asynchronous generator-iterator methods

This subsection describes the methods of an asynchronous generator iterator, which are used to control the execution of a generator function.

coroutine agen.__anext__()

>   Returns an awaitable which when run starts to execute the asynchronous generator or resumes it
>   at the last executed yield expression. When an asynchronous generator function is resumed with a
>   *__anext__ ()* method, the current yield expression always evaluates to **None** in the returned awaitable,
>   which when run will continue to the next yield expression. The value of the *expression_list* of
>   the yield expression is the value of the **StopIteration** exception raised by the completing coroutine.
>   If the asynchronous generator exits without yielding another value, the awaitable instead raises an
>   **StopAsyncIteration** exception, signalling that the asynchronous iteration has completed.
>
>   This method is normally called implicitly by a *async for* loop.

coroutine `agen.asend(`*value*`)`

Returns an awaitable which when run resumes the execution of the asynchronous generator. As with the *send()* method for a generator, this "sends" a value into the asynchronous generator function, and the *value* argument becomes the result of the current yield expression. The awaitable returned by the *asend()* method will return the next value yielded by the generator as the value of the raised `StopIteration`, or raises `StopAsyncIteration` if the asynchronous generator exits without yielding another value. When *asend()* is called to start the asynchronous generator, it must be called with `None` as the argument, because there is no yield expression that could receive the value.

coroutine `agen.athrow(`*type*`[, `*value*`[, `*traceback*`]])`

Returns an awaitable that raises an exception of type `type` at the point where the asynchronous generator was paused, and returns the next value yielded by the generator function as the value of the raised `StopIteration` exception. If the asynchronous generator exits without yielding another value, an `StopAsyncIteration` exception is raised by the awaitable. If the generator function does not catch the passed-in exception, or raises a different exception, then when the awaitable is run that exception propagates to the caller of the awaitable.

coroutine `agen.aclose()`

Returns an awaitable that when run will throw a `GeneratorExit` into the asynchronous generator function at the point where it was paused. If the asynchronous generator function then exits gracefully, is already closed, or raises `GeneratorExit` (by not catching the exception), then the returned awaitable will raise a `StopIteration` exception. Any further awaitables returned by subsequent calls to the asynchronous generator will raise a `StopAsyncIteration` exception. If the asynchronous generator yields a value, a `RuntimeError` is raised by the awaitable. If the asynchronous generator raises any other exception, it is propagated to the caller of the awaitable. If the asynchronous generator has already exited due to an exception or normal exit, then further calls to *aclose()* will return an awaitable that does nothing.

6.3 Primaries

Primaries represent the most tightly bound operations of the language. Their syntax is:

> `primary` ::= *atom* | *attributeref* | *subscription* | *slicing* | *call*

6.3.1 Attribute references

An attribute reference is a primary followed by a period and a name:

> `attributeref` ::= *primary* `"."` *identifier*

The primary must evaluate to an object of a type that supports attribute references, which most objects do. This object is then asked to produce the attribute whose name is the identifier. This production can be customized by overriding the *__getattr__()* method. If this attribute is not available, the exception `AttributeError` is raised. Otherwise, the type and value of the object produced is determined by the object. Multiple evaluations of the same attribute reference may yield different objects.

6.3.2 Subscriptions

A subscription selects an item of a sequence (string, tuple or list) or mapping (dictionary) object:

```
subscription  ::=   primary "[" expression_list "]"
```

The primary must evaluate to an object that supports subscription (lists or dictionaries for example). User-defined objects can support subscription by defining a `__getitem__()` method.

For built-in objects, there are two types of objects that support subscription:

If the primary is a mapping, the expression list must evaluate to an object whose value is one of the keys of the mapping, and the subscription selects the value in the mapping that corresponds to that key. (The expression list is a tuple except if it has exactly one item.)

If the primary is a sequence, the expression (list) must evaluate to an integer or a slice (as discussed in the following section).

The formal syntax makes no special provision for negative indices in sequences; however, built-in sequences all provide a `__getitem__()` method that interprets negative indices by adding the length of the sequence to the index (so that `x[-1]` selects the last item of `x`). The resulting value must be a nonnegative integer less than the number of items in the sequence, and the subscription selects the item whose index is that value (counting from zero). Since the support for negative indices and slicing occurs in the object's `__getitem__()` method, subclasses overriding this method will need to explicitly add that support.

A string's items are characters. A character is not a separate data type but a string of exactly one character.

6.3.3 Slicings

A slicing selects a range of items in a sequence object (e.g., a string, tuple or list). Slicings may be used as expressions or as targets in assignment or `del` statements. The syntax for a slicing:

```
slicing        ::=   primary "[" slice_list "]"
slice_list     ::=   slice_item ("," slice_item)* [","]
slice_item     ::=   expression | proper_slice
proper_slice   ::=   [lower_bound] ":" [upper_bound] [ ":" [stride] ]
lower_bound    ::=   expression
upper_bound    ::=   expression
stride         ::=   expression
```

There is ambiguity in the formal syntax here: anything that looks like an expression list also looks like a slice list, so any subscription can be interpreted as a slicing. Rather than further complicating the syntax, this is disambiguated by defining that in this case the interpretation as a subscription takes priority over the interpretation as a slicing (this is the case if the slice list contains no proper slice).

The semantics for a slicing are as follows. The primary is indexed (using the same `__getitem__()` method as normal subscription) with a key that is constructed from the slice list, as follows. If the slice list contains at least one comma, the key is a tuple containing the conversion of the slice items; otherwise, the conversion of the lone slice item is the key. The conversion of a slice item that is an expression is that expression. The conversion of a proper slice is a slice object (see section *The standard type hierarchy*) whose **start**, **stop** and **step** attributes are the values of the expressions given as lower bound, upper bound and stride, respectively, substituting **None** for missing expressions.

6.3.4 Calls

A call calls a callable object (e.g., a *function*) with a possibly empty series of *arguments*:

```
call                    ::=    primary "(" [argument_list [","] | comprehension] ")"
argument_list           ::=    positional_arguments ["," starred_and_keywords]
                               ["," keywords_arguments]
                               | starred_and_keywords ["," keywords_arguments]
                               | keywords_arguments
positional_arguments    ::=    ["*"] expression ("," ["*"] expression)*
starred_and_keywords    ::=    ("*" expression | keyword_item)
                               ("," "*" expression | "," keyword_item)*
keywords_arguments      ::=    (keyword_item | "**" expression)
                               ("," keyword_item | "," "**" expression)*
keyword_item            ::=    identifier "=" expression
```

An optional trailing comma may be present after the positional and keyword arguments but does not affect the semantics.

The primary must evaluate to a callable object (user-defined functions, built-in functions, methods of built-in objects, class objects, methods of class instances, and all objects having a _ _call_ _ () method are callable). All argument expressions are evaluated before the call is attempted. Please refer to section *Function defini-tions* for the syntax of formal *parameter* lists.

If keyword arguments are present, they are first converted to positional arguments, as follows. First, a list of unfilled slots is created for the formal parameters. If there are N positional arguments, they are placed in the first N slots. Next, for each keyword argument, the identifier is used to determine the corresponding slot (if the identifier is the same as the first formal parameter name, the first slot is used, and so on). If the slot is already filled, a `TypeError` exception is raised. Otherwise, the value of the argument is placed in the slot, filling it (even if the expression is `None`, it fills the slot). When all arguments have been processed, the slots that are still unfilled are filled with the corresponding default value from the function definition. (Default values are calculated, once, when the function is defined; thus, a mutable object such as a list or dictionary used as default value will be shared by all calls that don't specify an argument value for the corresponding slot; this should usually be avoided.) If there are any unfilled slots for which no default value is specified, a `TypeError` exception is raised. Otherwise, the list of filled slots is used as the argument list for the call.

CPython implementation detail: An implementation may provide built-in functions whose positional parameters do not have names, even if they are 'named' for the purpose of documentation, and which therefore cannot be supplied by keyword. In CPython, this is the case for functions implemented in C that use `PyArg_ParseTuple()` to parse their arguments.

If there are more positional arguments than there are formal parameter slots, a `TypeError` exception is raised, unless a formal parameter using the syntax `*identifier` is present; in this case, that formal parameter receives a tuple containing the excess positional arguments (or an empty tuple if there were no excess positional arguments).

If any keyword argument does not correspond to a formal parameter name, a `TypeError` exception is raised, unless a formal parameter using the syntax `**identifier` is present; in this case, that formal parameter receives a dictionary containing the excess keyword arguments (using the keywords as keys and the argument values as corresponding values), or a (new) empty dictionary if there were no excess keyword arguments.

If the syntax `*expression` appears in the function call, `expression` must evaluate to an *iterable*. Elements from these iterables are treated as if they were additional positional arguments. For the call f(x1, x2, *y, x3, x4), if *y* evaluates to a sequence *y1*, ..., *yM*, this is equivalent to a call with M+4 positional arguments *x1*, *x2*, *y1*, ..., *yM*, *x3*, *x4*.

A consequence of this is that although the `*expression` syntax may appear *after* explicit keyword arguments, it is processed *before* the keyword arguments (and any `**expression` arguments – see below). So:

```
>>> def f(a, b):
...     print(a, b)
```

```
...
>>> f(b=1, *(2,))
2 1
>>> f(a=1, *(2,))
Traceback (most recent call last):
  File "<stdin>", line 1, in <module>
TypeError: f() got multiple values for keyword argument 'a'
>>> f(1, *(2,))
1 2
```

It is unusual for both keyword arguments and the *expression syntax to be used in the same call, so in practice this confusion does not arise.

If the syntax **expression appears in the function call, expression must evaluate to a *mapping*, the contents of which are treated as additional keyword arguments. If a keyword is already present (as an explicit keyword argument, or from another unpacking), a TypeError exception is raised.

Formal parameters using the syntax *identifier or **identifier cannot be used as positional argument slots or as keyword argument names.

Changed in version 3.5: Function calls accept any number of * and ** unpackings, positional arguments may follow iterable unpackings (*), and keyword arguments may follow dictionary unpackings (**). Originally proposed by PEP 448.

A call always returns some value, possibly None, unless it raises an exception. How this value is computed depends on the type of the callable object.

If it is—

a user-defined function: The code block for the function is executed, passing it the argument list. The first thing the code block will do is bind the formal parameters to the arguments; this is described in section *Function definitions*. When the code block executes a *return* statement, this specifies the return value of the function call.

a built-in function or method: The result is up to the interpreter; see built-in-funcs for the descriptions of built-in functions and methods.

a class object: A new instance of that class is returned.

a class instance method: The corresponding user-defined function is called, with an argument list that is one longer than the argument list of the call: the instance becomes the first argument.

a class instance: The class must define a `__call__()` method; the effect is then the same as if that method was called.

6.4 Await expression

Suspend the execution of *coroutine* on an *awaitable* object. Can only be used inside a *coroutine function*.

```
await_expr ::= "await" primary
```

New in version 3.5.

6.5 The power operator

The power operator binds more tightly than unary operators on its left; it binds less tightly than unary operators on its right. The syntax is:

```
power    ::=   ( await_expr | primary ) ["**" u_expr]
```

Thus, in an unparenthesized sequence of power and unary operators, the operators are evaluated from right to left (this does not constrain the evaluation order for the operands): `-1**2` results in `-1`.

The power operator has the same semantics as the built-in `pow()` function, when called with two arguments: it yields its left argument raised to the power of its right argument. The numeric arguments are first converted to a common type, and the result is of that type.

For int operands, the result has the same type as the operands unless the second argument is negative; in that case, all arguments are converted to float and a float result is delivered. For example, `10**2` returns 100, but `10**-2` returns 0.01.

Raising 0.0 to a negative power results in a `ZeroDivisionError`. Raising a negative number to a fractional power results in a `complex` number. (In earlier versions it raised a `ValueError`.)

6.6 Unary arithmetic and bitwise operations

All unary arithmetic and bitwise operations have the same priority:

```
u_expr   ::=   power | "-" u_expr | "+" u_expr | "~" u_expr
```

The unary - (minus) operator yields the negation of its numeric argument.

The unary + (plus) operator yields its numeric argument unchanged.

The unary ~ (invert) operator yields the bitwise inversion of its integer argument. The bitwise inversion of x is defined as `-(x+1)`. It only applies to integral numbers.

In all three cases, if the argument does not have the proper type, a `TypeError` exception is raised.

6.7 Binary arithmetic operations

The binary arithmetic operations have the conventional priority levels. Note that some of these operations also apply to certain non-numeric types. Apart from the power operator, there are only two levels, one for multiplicative operators and one for additive operators:

```
m_expr   ::=   u_expr | m_expr "*" u_expr | m_expr "@" m_expr |
               m_expr "//" u_expr| m_expr "/" u_expr |
               m_expr "%" u_expr
a_expr   ::=   m_expr | a_expr "+" m_expr | a_expr "-" m_expr
```

The * (multiplication) operator yields the product of its arguments. The arguments must either both be numbers, or one argument must be an integer and the other must be a sequence. In the former case, the numbers are converted to a common type and then multiplied together. In the latter case, sequence repetition is performed; a negative repetition factor yields an empty sequence.

The @ (at) operator is intended to be used for matrix multiplication. No builtin Python types implement this operator.

New in version 3.5.

The / (division) and // (floor division) operators yield the quotient of their arguments. The numeric arguments are first converted to a common type. Division of integers yields a float, while floor division of integers results in an integer; the result is that of mathematical division with the 'floor' function applied to the result. Division by zero raises the `ZeroDivisionError` exception.

The % (modulo) operator yields the remainder from the division of the first argument by the second. The numeric arguments are first converted to a common type. A zero right argument raises the `ZeroDivisionError` exception. The arguments may be floating point numbers, e.g., `3.14%0.7` equals `0.34` (since `3.14` equals `4*0.7 + 0.34`.) The modulo operator always yields a result with the same sign as its second operand (or zero); the absolute value of the result is strictly smaller than the absolute value of the second operand[1].

The floor division and modulo operators are connected by the following identity: `x == (x//y)*y + (x%y)`. Floor division and modulo are also connected with the built-in function `divmod()`: `divmod(x, y) == (x//y, x%y)`.[2].

In addition to performing the modulo operation on numbers, the % operator is also overloaded by string objects to perform old-style string formatting (also known as interpolation). The syntax for string formatting is described in the Python Library Reference, section old-string-formatting.

The floor division operator, the modulo operator, and the `divmod()` function are not defined for complex numbers. Instead, convert to a floating point number using the `abs()` function if appropriate.

The + (addition) operator yields the sum of its arguments. The arguments must either both be numbers or both be sequences of the same type. In the former case, the numbers are converted to a common type and then added together. In the latter case, the sequences are concatenated.

The - (subtraction) operator yields the difference of its arguments. The numeric arguments are first converted to a common type.

6.8 Shifting operations

The shifting operations have lower priority than the arithmetic operations:

```
shift_expr   ::=   a_expr | shift_expr ( "<<" | ">>" ) a_expr
```

These operators accept integers as arguments. They shift the first argument to the left or right by the number of bits given by the second argument.

A right shift by n bits is defined as floor division by `pow(2,n)`. A left shift by n bits is defined as multiplication with `pow(2,n)`.

Note: In the current implementation, the right-hand operand is required to be at most `sys.maxsize`. If the right-hand operand is larger than `sys.maxsize` an `OverflowError` exception is raised.

---

[1] While `abs(x%y) < abs(y)` is true mathematically, for floats it may not be true numerically due to roundoff. For example, and assuming a platform on which a Python float is an IEEE 754 double-precision number, in order that `-1e-100 % 1e100` have the same sign as `1e100`, the computed result is `-1e-100 + 1e100`, which is numerically exactly equal to `1e100`. The function `math.fmod()` returns a result whose sign matches the sign of the first argument instead, and so returns `-1e-100` in this case. Which approach is more appropriate depends on the application.

[2] If x is very close to an exact integer multiple of y, it's possible for `x//y` to be one larger than `(x-x%y)//y` due to rounding. In such cases, Python returns the latter result, in order to preserve that `divmod(x,y)[0] * y + x % y` be very close to x.

6.9 Binary bitwise operations

Each of the three bitwise operations has a different priority level:

```
and_expr   ::=   shift_expr | and_expr "&" shift_expr
xor_expr   ::=   and_expr | xor_expr "^" and_expr
or_expr    ::=   xor_expr | or_expr "|" xor_expr
```

The & operator yields the bitwise AND of its arguments, which must be integers.

The ^ operator yields the bitwise XOR (exclusive OR) of its arguments, which must be integers.

The | operator yields the bitwise (inclusive) OR of its arguments, which must be integers.

6.10 Comparisons

Unlike C, all comparison operations in Python have the same priority, which is lower than that of any arithmetic, shifting or bitwise operation. Also unlike C, expressions like a < b < c have the interpretation that is conventional in mathematics:

```
comparison      ::=   or_expr ( comp_operator or_expr )*
comp_operator   ::=   "<" | ">" | "==" | ">=" | "<=" | "!="
                      | "is" ["not"] | ["not"] "in"
```

Comparisons yield boolean values: True or False.

Comparisons can be chained arbitrarily, e.g., x < y <= z is equivalent to x < y and y <= z, except that y is evaluated only once (but in both cases z is not evaluated at all when x < y is found to be false).

Formally, if *a*, *b*, *c*, ..., *y*, *z* are expressions and *op1*, *op2*, ..., *opN* are comparison operators, then a op1 b op2 c ... y opN z is equivalent to a op1 b and b op2 c and ... y opN z, except that each expression is evaluated at most once.

Note that a op1 b op2 c doesn't imply any kind of comparison between *a* and *c*, so that, e.g., x < y > z is perfectly legal (though perhaps not pretty).

6.10.1 Value comparisons

The operators <, >, ==, >=, <=, and != compare the values of two objects. The objects do not need to have the same type.

Chapter *Objects, values and types* states that objects have a value (in addition to type and identity). The value of an object is a rather abstract notion in Python: For example, there is no canonical access method for an object's value. Also, there is no requirement that the value of an object should be constructed in a particular way, e.g. comprised of all its data attributes. Comparison operators implement a particular notion of what the value of an object is. One can think of them as defining the value of an object indirectly, by means of their comparison implementation.

Because all types are (direct or indirect) subtypes of object, they inherit the default comparison behavior from object. Types can customize their comparison behavior by implementing *rich comparison methods* like __lt__(), described in *Basic customization*.

The default behavior for equality comparison (== and !=) is based on the identity of the objects. Hence, equality comparison of instances with the same identity results in equality, and equality comparison of instances with different identities results in inequality. A motivation for this default behavior is the desire that all objects should be reflexive (i.e. `x is y` implies `x == y`).

A default order comparison (`<`, `>`, `<=`, and `>=`) is not provided; an attempt raises `TypeError`. A motivation for this default behavior is the lack of a similar invariant as for equality.

The behavior of the default equality comparison, that instances with different identities are always unequal, may be in contrast to what types will need that have a sensible definition of object value and value-based equality. Such types will need to customize their comparison behavior, and in fact, a number of built-in types have done that.

The following list describes the comparison behavior of the most important built-in types.

- Numbers of built-in numeric types (typesnumeric) and of the standard library types `fractions.Fraction` and `decimal.Decimal` can be compared within and across their types, with the restriction that complex numbers do not support order comparison. Within the limits of the types involved, they compare mathematically (algorithmically) correct without loss of precision.

  The not-a-number values `float('NaN')` and `Decimal('NaN')` are special. They are identical to themselves (`x is x` is true) but are not equal to themselves (`x == x` is false). Additionally, comparing any number to a not-a-number value will return `False`. For example, both `3 < float('NaN')` and `float('NaN') < 3` will return `False`.

- Binary sequences (instances of `bytes` or `bytearray`) can be compared within and across their types. They compare lexicographically using the numeric values of their elements.

- Strings (instances of `str`) compare lexicographically using the numerical Unicode code points (the result of the built-in function `ord()`) of their characters.[3]

  Strings and binary sequences cannot be directly compared.

- Sequences (instances of `tuple`, `list`, or `range`) can be compared only within each of their types, with the restriction that ranges do not support order comparison. Equality comparison across these types results in inequality, and ordering comparison across these types raises `TypeError`.

  Sequences compare lexicographically using comparison of corresponding elements, whereby reflexivity of the elements is enforced.

  In enforcing reflexivity of elements, the comparison of collections assumes that for a collection element x, `x == x` is always true. Based on that assumption, element identity is compared first, and element comparison is performed only for distinct elements. This approach yields the same result as a strict element comparison would, if the compared elements are reflexive. For non-reflexive elements, the result is different than for strict element comparison, and may be surprising: The non-reflexive not-a-number values for example result in the following comparison behavior when used in a list:

```
>>> nan = float('NaN')
>>> nan is nan
True
>>> nan == nan
False                   <-- the defined non-reflexive behavior of NaN
>>> [nan] == [nan]
True                    <-- list enforces reflexivity and tests identity first
```

---

[3] The Unicode standard distinguishes between *code points* (e.g. U+0041) and *abstract characters* (e.g. "LATIN CAPITAL LETTER A"). While most abstract characters in Unicode are only represented using one code point, there is a number of abstract characters that can in addition be represented using a sequence of more than one code point. For example, the abstract character "LATIN CAPITAL LETTER C WITH CEDILLA" can be represented as a single *precomposed character* at code position U+00C7, or as a sequence of a *base character* at code position U+0043 (LATIN CAPITAL LETTER C), followed by a *combining character* at code position U+0327 (COMBINING CEDILLA).

The comparison operators on strings compare at the level of Unicode code points. This may be counter-intuitive to humans. For example, `"\u00C7" == "\u0043\u0327"` is `False`, even though both strings represent the same abstract character "LATIN CAPITAL LETTER C WITH CEDILLA".

To compare strings at the level of abstract characters (that is, in a way intuitive to humans), use `unicodedata.normalize()`.

Lexicographical comparison between built-in collections works as follows:

- For two collections to compare equal, they must be of the same type, have the same length, and each pair of corresponding elements must compare equal (for example, [1,2] == (1,2) is false because the type is not the same).

- Collections that support order comparison are ordered the same as their first unequal elements (for example, [1,2,x] <= [1,2,y] has the same value as x <= y). If a corresponding element does not exist, the shorter collection is ordered first (for example, [1,2] < [1,2,3] is true).

- Mappings (instances of dict) compare equal if and only if they have equal *(key, value)* pairs. Equality comparison of the keys and values enforces reflexivity.

  Order comparisons (<, >, <=, and >=) raise TypeError.

- Sets (instances of set or frozenset) can be compared within and across their types.

  They define order comparison operators to mean subset and superset tests. Those relations do not define total orderings (for example, the two sets {1,2} and {2,3} are not equal, nor subsets of one another, nor supersets of one another). Accordingly, sets are not appropriate arguments for functions which depend on total ordering (for example, min(), max(), and sorted() produce undefined results given a list of sets as inputs).

  Comparison of sets enforces reflexivity of its elements.

- Most other built-in types have no comparison methods implemented, so they inherit the default comparison behavior.

User-defined classes that customize their comparison behavior should follow some consistency rules, if possible:

- Equality comparison should be reflexive. In other words, identical objects should compare equal:

  x is y implies x == y

- Comparison should be symmetric. In other words, the following expressions should have the same result:

  x == y and y == x

  x != y and y != x

  x < y and y > x

  x <= y and y >= x

- Comparison should be transitive. The following (non-exhaustive) examples illustrate that:

  x > y and y > z implies x > z

  x < y and y <= z implies x < z

- Inverse comparison should result in the boolean negation. In other words, the following expressions should have the same result:

  x == y and not x != y

  x < y and not x >= y (for total ordering)

  x > y and not x <= y (for total ordering)

  The last two expressions apply to totally ordered collections (e.g. to sequences, but not to sets or mappings). See also the total_ordering() decorator.

- The hash() result should be consistent with equality. Objects that are equal should either have the same hash value, or be marked as unhashable.

Python does not enforce these consistency rules. In fact, the not-a-number values are an example for not following these rules.

6.10.2 Membership test operations

The operators *in* and *not in* test for membership. `x in s` evaluates to `True` if x is a member of s, and `False` otherwise. `x not in s` returns the negation of `x in s`. All built-in sequences and set types support this as well as dictionary, for which *in* tests whether the dictionary has a given key. For container types such as list, tuple, set, frozenset, dict, or collections.deque, the expression `x in y` is equivalent to `any(x is e or x == e for e in y)`.

For the string and bytes types, `x in y` is `True` if and only if x is a substring of y. An equivalent test is `y.find(x) != -1`. Empty strings are always considered to be a substring of any other string, so `"" in "abc"` will return `True`.

For user-defined classes which define the *__contains__()* method, `x in y` returns `True` if `y.__contains__(x)` returns a true value, and `False` otherwise.

For user-defined classes which do not define *__contains__()* but do define *__iter__()*, `x in y` is `True` if some value `z` with `x == z` is produced while iterating over `y`. If an exception is raised during the iteration, it is as if *in* raised that exception.

Lastly, the old-style iteration protocol is tried: if a class defines *__getitem__()*, `x in y` is `True` if and only if there is a non-negative integer index i such that `x == y[i]`, and all lower integer indices do not raise `IndexError` exception. (If any other exception is raised, it is as if *in* raised that exception).

The operator *not in* is defined to have the inverse true value of *in*.

6.10.3 Identity comparisons

The operators *is* and *is not* test for object identity: `x is y` is true if and only if x and y are the same object. Object identity is determined using the `id()` function. `x is not y` yields the inverse truth value.[4]

6.11 Boolean operations

```
or_test    ::=    and_test | or_test "or" and_test
and_test   ::=    not_test | and_test "and" not_test
not_test   ::=    comparison | "not" not_test
```

In the context of Boolean operations, and also when expressions are used by control flow statements, the following values are interpreted as false: `False`, `None`, numeric zero of all types, and empty strings and containers (including strings, tuples, lists, dictionaries, sets and frozensets). All other values are interpreted as true. User-defined objects can customize their truth value by providing a *__bool__()* method.

The operator *not* yields `True` if its argument is false, `False` otherwise.

The expression `x and y` first evaluates x; if x is false, its value is returned; otherwise, y is evaluated and the resulting value is returned.

The expression `x or y` first evaluates x; if x is true, its value is returned; otherwise, y is evaluated and the resulting value is returned.

(Note that neither *and* nor *or* restrict the value and type they return to `False` and `True`, but rather return the last evaluated argument. This is sometimes useful, e.g., if `s` is a string that should be replaced by a default value if it is empty, the expression `s or 'foo'` yields the desired value. Because *not* has to create a new value, it returns a boolean value regardless of the type of its argument (for example, `not 'foo'` produces `False` rather than `''`.)

---

[4] Due to automatic garbage-collection, free lists, and the dynamic nature of descriptors, you may notice seemingly unusual behaviour in certain uses of the *is* operator, like those involving comparisons between instance methods, or constants. Check their documentation for more info.

6.12 Conditional expressions

```
conditional_expression  ::=   or_test ["if" or_test "else" expression]
expression               ::=   conditional_expression | lambda_expr
expression_nocond        ::=   or_test | lambda_expr_nocond
```

Conditional expressions (sometimes called a "ternary operator") have the lowest priority of all Python operations.

The expression x if C else y first evaluates the condition, C rather than x. If C is true, x is evaluated and its value is returned; otherwise, y is evaluated and its value is returned.

See PEP 308 for more details about conditional expressions.

6.13 Lambdas

```
lambda_expr          ::=   "lambda" [parameter_list]: expression
lambda_expr_nocond   ::=   "lambda" [parameter_list]: expression_nocond
```

Lambda expressions (sometimes called lambda forms) are used to create anonymous functions. The expression lambda arguments: expression yields a function object. The unnamed object behaves like a function object defined with:

```
def <lambda>(arguments):
    return expression
```

See section *Function definitions* for the syntax of parameter lists. Note that functions created with lambda expressions cannot contain statements or annotations.

6.14 Expression lists

```
expression_list      ::=   expression ( "," expression )* [","]
starred_list         ::=   starred_item ( "," starred_item )* [","]
starred_expression   ::=   expression | ( starred_item "," )* [starred_item]
starred_item         ::=   expression | "*" or_expr
```

Except when part of a list or set display, an expression list containing at least one comma yields a tuple. The length of the tuple is the number of expressions in the list. The expressions are evaluated from left to right.

An asterisk * denotes *iterable unpacking*. Its operand must be an *iterable*. The iterable is expanded into a sequence of items, which are included in the new tuple, list, or set, at the site of the unpacking.

New in version 3.5: Iterable unpacking in expression lists, originally proposed by PEP 448.

The trailing comma is required only to create a single tuple (a.k.a. a *singleton*); it is optional in all other cases. A single expression without a trailing comma doesn't create a tuple, but rather yields the value of that expression. (To create an empty tuple, use an empty pair of parentheses: ().)

6.15 Evaluation order

Python evaluates expressions from left to right. Notice that while evaluating an assignment, the right-hand side is evaluated before the left-hand side.

In the following lines, expressions will be evaluated in the arithmetic order of their suffixes:

```
expr1, expr2, expr3, expr4
(expr1, expr2, expr3, expr4)
{expr1: expr2, expr3: expr4}
expr1 + expr2 * (expr3 - expr4)
expr1(expr2, expr3, *expr4, **expr5)
expr3, expr4 = expr1, expr2
```

6.16 Operator precedence

The following table summarizes the operator precedence in Python, from lowest precedence (least binding) to highest precedence (most binding). Operators in the same box have the same precedence. Unless the syntax is explicitly given, operators are binary. Operators in the same box group left to right (except for exponentiation, which groups from right to left).

Note that comparisons, membership tests, and identity tests, all have the same precedence and have a left-to-right chaining feature as described in the *Comparisons* section.

Operator	Description
lambda	Lambda expression
if − else	Conditional expression
or	Boolean OR
and	Boolean AND
not x	Boolean NOT
in, not in, is, is not, <, <=, >, >=, !=, ==	Comparisons, including membership tests and identity tests
|	Bitwise OR
^	Bitwise XOR
&	Bitwise AND
<<, >>	Shifts
+, -	Addition and subtraction
*, @, /, //, %	Multiplication, matrix multiplication, division, floor division, remainder[5]
+x, -x, ~x	Positive, negative, bitwise NOT
**	Exponentiation[6]
await x	Await expression
x[index], x[index:index], x(arguments...), x.attribute	Subscription, slicing, call, attribute reference
(expressions...), [expressions...], {key: value...}, {expressions...}	Binding or tuple display, list display, dictionary display, set display

[5] The % operator is also used for string formatting; the same precedence applies.
[6] The power operator ** binds less tightly than an arithmetic or bitwise unary operator on its right, that is, 2**-1 is 0.5.

SIMPLE STATEMENTS

A simple statement is comprised within a single logical line. Several simple statements may occur on a single line separated by semicolons. The syntax for simple statements is:

```
simple_stmt  ::=   expression_stmt
               |  assert_stmt
               |  assignment_stmt
               |  augmented_assignment_stmt
               |  annotated_assignment_stmt
               |  pass_stmt
               |  del_stmt
               |  return_stmt
               |  yield_stmt
               |  raise_stmt
               |  break_stmt
               |  continue_stmt
               |  import_stmt
               |  global_stmt
               |  nonlocal_stmt
```

7.1 Expression statements

Expression statements are used (mostly interactively) to compute and write a value, or (usually) to call a procedure (a function that returns no meaningful result; in Python, procedures return the value None). Other uses of expression statements are allowed and occasionally useful. The syntax for an expression statement is:

```
expression_stmt  ::=   starred_expression
```

An expression statement evaluates the expression list (which may be a single expression).

In interactive mode, if the value is not None, it is converted to a string using the built-in repr() function and the resulting string is written to standard output on a line by itself (except if the result is None, so that procedure calls do not cause any output.)

7.2 Assignment statements

Assignment statements are used to (re)bind names to values and to modify attributes or items of mutable objects:

```
assignment_stmt  ::=  (target_list "=")+ (starred_expression | yield_expression)
target_list      ::=  target ("," target)* [","]
target           ::=  identifier
                      | "(" [target_list] ")"
                      | "[" [target_list] "]"
                      | attributeref
                      | subscription
                      | slicing
                      | "*" target
```

(See section *Primaries* for the syntax definitions for *attributeref*, *subscription*, and *slicing*.)

An assignment statement evaluates the expression list (remember that this can be a single expression or a comma-separated list, the latter yielding a tuple) and assigns the single resulting object to each of the target lists, from left to right.

Assignment is defined recursively depending on the form of the target (list). When a target is part of a mutable object (an attribute reference, subscription or slicing), the mutable object must ultimately perform the assignment and decide about its validity, and may raise an exception if the assignment is unacceptable. The rules observed by various types and the exceptions raised are given with the definition of the object types (see section *The standard type hierarchy*).

Assignment of an object to a target list, optionally enclosed in parentheses or square brackets, is recursively defined as follows.

- If the target list is empty: The object must also be an empty iterable.

- If the target list is a single target in parentheses: The object is assigned to that target.

- If the target list is a comma-separated list of targets, or a single target in square brackets: The object must be an iterable with the same number of items as there are targets in the target list, and the items are assigned, from left to right, to the corresponding targets.

  - If the target list contains one target prefixed with an asterisk, called a "starred" target: The object must be an iterable with at least as many items as there are targets in the target list, minus one. The first items of the iterable are assigned, from left to right, to the targets before the starred target. The final items of the iterable are assigned to the targets after the starred target. A list of the remaining items in the iterable is then assigned to the starred target (the list can be empty).

  - Else: The object must be an iterable with the same number of items as there are targets in the target list, and the items are assigned, from left to right, to the corresponding targets.

Assignment of an object to a single target is recursively defined as follows.

- If the target is an identifier (name):

  - If the name does not occur in a *global* or *nonlocal* statement in the current code block: the name is bound to the object in the current local namespace.

  - Otherwise: the name is bound to the object in the global namespace or the outer namespace determined by *nonlocal*, respectively.

  The name is rebound if it was already bound. This may cause the reference count for the object previously bound to the name to reach zero, causing the object to be deallocated and its destructor (if it has one) to be called.

- If the target is an attribute reference: The primary expression in the reference is evaluated. It should yield an object with assignable attributes; if this is not the case, `TypeError` is raised. That object is then asked to assign the assigned object to the given attribute; if it cannot perform the assignment, it raises an exception (usually but not necessarily `AttributeError`). Note: If the object is a class instance and the attribute reference occurs on both sides of the assignment operator, the RHS expression, `a.x` can access either an instance attribute or (if no instance attribute exists) a class attribute. The LHS target `a.x` is always set as an instance attribute, creating it if necessary. Thus, the two occurrences of `a.x` do not necessarily refer to the same attribute: if the RHS expression refers to a class attribute, the LHS creates a new instance attribute as the target of the assignment:

```
class Cls:
    x = 3               # class variable
inst = Cls()
inst.x = inst.x + 1    # writes inst.x as 4 leaving Cls.x as 3
```

This description does not necessarily apply to descriptor attributes, such as properties created with `property()`.

- If the target is a subscription: The primary expression in the reference is evaluated. It should yield either a mutable sequence object (such as a list) or a mapping object (such as a dictionary). Next, the subscript expression is evaluated.

  If the primary is a mutable sequence object (such as a list), the subscript must yield an integer. If it is negative, the sequence's length is added to it. The resulting value must be a nonnegative integer less than the sequence's length, and the sequence is asked to assign the assigned object to its item with that index. If the index is out of range, `IndexError` is raised (assignment to a subscripted sequence cannot add new items to a list).

  If the primary is a mapping object (such as a dictionary), the subscript must have a type compatible with the mapping's key type, and the mapping is then asked to create a key/datum pair which maps the subscript to the assigned object. This can either replace an existing key/value pair with the same key value, or insert a new key/value pair (if no key with the same value existed).

  For user-defined objects, the `__setitem__()` method is called with appropriate arguments.

- If the target is a slicing: The primary expression in the reference is evaluated. It should yield a mutable sequence object (such as a list). The assigned object should be a sequence object of the same type. Next, the lower and upper bound expressions are evaluated, insofar they are present; defaults are zero and the sequence's length. The bounds should evaluate to integers. If either bound is negative, the sequence's length is added to it. The resulting bounds are clipped to lie between zero and the sequence's length, inclusive. Finally, the sequence object is asked to replace the slice with the items of the assigned sequence. The length of the slice may be different from the length of the assigned sequence, thus changing the length of the target sequence, if the target sequence allows it.

CPython implementation detail: In the current implementation, the syntax for targets is taken to be the same as for expressions, and invalid syntax is rejected during the code generation phase, causing less detailed error messages.

Although the definition of assignment implies that overlaps between the left-hand side and the right-hand side are 'simultaneous' (for example `a, b = b, a` swaps two variables), overlaps *within* the collection of assigned-to variables occur left-to-right, sometimes resulting in confusion. For instance, the following program prints [0, 2]:

```
x = [0, 1]
i = 0
i, x[i] = 1, 2          # i is updated, then x[i] is updated
print(x)
```

See also:

PEP 3132 - **Extended Iterable Unpacking** The specification for the `*target` feature.

7.2.1 Augmented assignment statements

Augmented assignment is the combination, in a single statement, of a binary operation and an assignment statement:

`augmented_assignment_stmt`	::=	*augtarget augop* (*expression_list* | *yield_expression*)
`augtarget`	::=	*identifier* | *attributeref* | *subscription* | *slicing*
`augop`	::=	`"+="` | `"-="` | `"*="` | `"@="` | `"/="` | `"//="` | `"%="` | `"**="`
		| `">>="` | `"<<="` | `"&="` | `"^="` | `"|="`

(See section *Primaries* for the syntax definitions of the last three symbols.)

An augmented assignment evaluates the target (which, unlike normal assignment statements, cannot be an unpacking) and the expression list, performs the binary operation specific to the type of assignment on the two operands, and assigns the result to the original target. The target is only evaluated once.

An augmented assignment expression like `x += 1` can be rewritten as `x = x + 1` to achieve a similar, but not exactly equal effect. In the augmented version, `x` is only evaluated once. Also, when possible, the actual operation is performed *in-place*, meaning that rather than creating a new object and assigning that to the target, the old object is modified instead.

Unlike normal assignments, augmented assignments evaluate the left-hand side *before* evaluating the right-hand side. For example, `a[i] += f(x)` first looks-up `a[i]`, then it evaluates `f(x)` and performs the addition, and lastly, it writes the result back to `a[i]`.

With the exception of assigning to tuples and multiple targets in a single statement, the assignment done by augmented assignment statements is handled the same way as normal assignments. Similarly, with the exception of the possible *in-place* behavior, the binary operation performed by augmented assignment is the same as the normal binary operations.

For targets which are attribute references, the same *caveat about class and instance attributes* applies as for regular assignments.

7.2.2 Annotated assignment statements

Annotation assignment is the combination, in a single statement, of a variable or attribute annotation and an optional assignment statement:

`annotated_assignment_stmt`	::=	*augtarget* `":"` *expression* [`"="` *expression*]

The difference from normal *Assignment statements* is that only single target and only single right hand side value is allowed.

For simple names as assignment targets, if in class or module scope, the annotations are evaluated and stored in a special class or module attribute `__annotations__` that is a dictionary mapping from variable names (mangled if private) to evaluated annotations. This attribute is writable and is automatically created at the start of class or module body execution, if annotations are found statically.

For expressions as assignment targets, the annotations are evaluated if in class or module scope, but not stored.

If a name is annotated in a function scope, then this name is local for that scope. Annotations are never evaluated and stored in function scopes.

If the right hand side is present, an annotated assignment performs the actual assignment before evaluating annotations (where applicable). If the right hand side is not present for an expression target, then the interpreter evaluates the target except for the last *__setitem__ ()* or *__setattr__ ()* call.

See also:

PEP 526 - Variable and attribute annotation syntax PEP 484 - Type hints

7.3 The `assert` statement

Assert statements are a convenient way to insert debugging assertions into a program:

```
assert_stmt  ::=   "assert" expression ["," expression]
```

The simple form, `assert expression`, is equivalent to

```
if __debug__:
    if not expression: raise AssertionError
```

The extended form, `assert expression1, expression2`, is equivalent to

```
if __debug__:
    if not expression1: raise AssertionError(expression2)
```

These equivalences assume that `__debug__` and `AssertionError` refer to the built-in variables with those names. In the current implementation, the built-in variable `__debug__` is `True` under normal circumstances, `False` when optimization is requested (command line option -O). The current code generator emits no code for an assert statement when optimization is requested at compile time. Note that it is unnecessary to include the source code for the expression that failed in the error message; it will be displayed as part of the stack trace.

Assignments to `__debug__` are illegal. The value for the built-in variable is determined when the interpreter starts.

7.4 The `pass` statement

```
pass_stmt  ::=   "pass"
```

pass is a null operation — when it is executed, nothing happens. It is useful as a placeholder when a statement is required syntactically, but no code needs to be executed, for example:

```
def f(arg): pass    # a function that does nothing (yet)

class C: pass       # a class with no methods (yet)
```

7.5 The `del` statement

```
del_stmt  ::=   "del" target_list
```

Deletion is recursively defined very similar to the way assignment is defined. Rather than spelling it out in full details, here are some hints.

Deletion of a target list recursively deletes each target, from left to right.

Deletion of a name removes the binding of that name from the local or global namespace, depending on whether the name occurs in a *global* statement in the same code block. If the name is unbound, a `NameError` exception will be raised.

Deletion of attribute references, subscriptions and slicings is passed to the primary object involved; deletion of a slicing is in general equivalent to assignment of an empty slice of the right type (but even this is determined by the sliced object).

Changed in version 3.2: Previously it was illegal to delete a name from the local namespace if it occurs as a free variable in a nested block.

7.6 The `return` statement

> return_stmt   ::=   "return" [*expression_list*]

return may only occur syntactically nested in a function definition, not within a nested class definition.

If an expression list is present, it is evaluated, else `None` is substituted.

return leaves the current function call with the expression list (or `None`) as return value.

When *return* passes control out of a *try* statement with a *finally* clause, that *finally* clause is executed before really leaving the function.

In a generator function, the *return* statement indicates that the generator is done and will cause `StopIteration` to be raised. The returned value (if any) is used as an argument to construct `StopIteration` and becomes the `StopIteration.value` attribute.

In an asynchronous generator function, an empty *return* statement indicates that the asynchronous generator is done and will cause `StopAsyncIteration` to be raised. A non-empty *return* statement is a syntax error in an asynchronous generator function.

7.7 The `yield` statement

> yield_stmt   ::=   *yield_expression*

A *yield* statement is semantically equivalent to a *yield expression*. The yield statement can be used to omit the parentheses that would otherwise be required in the equivalent yield expression statement. For example, the yield statements

```
yield <expr>
yield from <expr>
```

are equivalent to the yield expression statements

```
(yield <expr>)
(yield from <expr>)
```

Yield expressions and statements are only used when defining a *generator* function, and are only used in the body of the generator function. Using yield in a function definition is sufficient to cause that definition to create a generator function instead of a normal function.

For full details of *yield* semantics, refer to the *Yield expressions* section.

7.8 The `raise` statement

```
raise_stmt  ::=  "raise" [expression ["from" expression]]
```

If no expressions are present, *raise* re-raises the last exception that was active in the current scope. If no exception is active in the current scope, a **RuntimeError** exception is raised indicating that this is an error.

Otherwise, *raise* evaluates the first expression as the exception object. It must be either a subclass or an instance of **BaseException**. If it is a class, the exception instance will be obtained when needed by instantiating the class with no arguments.

The *type* of the exception is the exception instance's class, the *value* is the instance itself.

A traceback object is normally created automatically when an exception is raised and attached to it as the `__traceback__` attribute, which is writable. You can create an exception and set your own traceback in one step using the `with_traceback()` exception method (which returns the same exception instance, with its traceback set to its argument), like so:

```
raise Exception("foo occurred").with_traceback(tracebackobj)
```

The **from** clause is used for exception chaining: if given, the second *expression* must be another exception class or instance, which will then be attached to the raised exception as the `__cause__` attribute (which is writable). If the raised exception is not handled, both exceptions will be printed:

```
>>> try:
...     print(1 / 0)
... except Exception as exc:
...     raise RuntimeError("Something bad happened") from exc
...
Traceback (most recent call last):
  File "<stdin>", line 2, in <module>
ZeroDivisionError: division by zero

The above exception was the direct cause of the following exception:

Traceback (most recent call last):
  File "<stdin>", line 4, in <module>
RuntimeError: Something bad happened
```

A similar mechanism works implicitly if an exception is raised inside an exception handler or a *finally* clause: the previous exception is then attached as the new exception's `__context__` attribute:

```
>>> try:
...     print(1 / 0)
... except:
...     raise RuntimeError("Something bad happened")
...
Traceback (most recent call last):
  File "<stdin>", line 2, in <module>
ZeroDivisionError: division by zero

During handling of the above exception, another exception occurred:

Traceback (most recent call last):
```

```
  File "<stdin>", line 4, in <module>
RuntimeError: Something bad happened
```

Exception chaining can be explicitly suppressed by specifying None in the from clause:

```
>>> try:
...     print(1 / 0)
... except:
...     raise RuntimeError("Something bad happened") from None
...
Traceback (most recent call last):
  File "<stdin>", line 4, in <module>
RuntimeError: Something bad happened
```

Additional information on exceptions can be found in section *Exceptions*, and information about handling exceptions is in section *The try statement*.

Changed in version 3.3: None is now permitted as Y in raise X from Y.

New in version 3.3: The __suppress_context__ attribute to suppress automatic display of the exception context.

7.9 The break statement

```
break_stmt   ::=   "break"
```

break may only occur syntactically nested in a *for* or *while* loop, but not nested in a function or class definition within that loop.

It terminates the nearest enclosing loop, skipping the optional *else* clause if the loop has one.

If a *for* loop is terminated by *break*, the loop control target keeps its current value.

When *break* passes control out of a *try* statement with a *finally* clause, that *finally* clause is executed before really leaving the loop.

7.10 The continue statement

```
continue_stmt   ::=   "continue"
```

continue may only occur syntactically nested in a *for* or *while* loop, but not nested in a function or class definition or *finally* clause within that loop. It continues with the next cycle of the nearest enclosing loop.

When *continue* passes control out of a *try* statement with a *finally* clause, that *finally* clause is executed before really starting the next loop cycle.

7.11 The import statement

```
import_stmt      ::=    "import" module ["as" name] ( "," module ["as" name] )*
                    | "from" relative_module "import" identifier ["as" name]
                    ( "," identifier ["as" name] )*
                    | "from" relative_module "import" "(" identifier ["as" name]
```

```
                          ( "," identifier ["as" name] )* [","] ")"
                          | "from" module "import" "*"
module            ::=     (identifier ".")* identifier
relative_module   ::=     "."* module | "."+
name              ::=     identifier
```

The basic import statement (no *from* clause) is executed in two steps:

1. find a module, loading and initializing it if necessary

2. define a name or names in the local namespace for the scope where the *import* statement occurs.

When the statement contains multiple clauses (separated by commas) the two steps are carried out separately for each clause, just as though the clauses had been separated out into individual import statements.

The details of the first step, finding and loading modules are described in greater detail in the section on the *import system*, which also describes the various types of packages and modules that can be imported, as well as all the hooks that can be used to customize the import system. Note that failures in this step may indicate either that the module could not be located, *or* that an error occurred while initializing the module, which includes execution of the module's code.

If the requested module is retrieved successfully, it will be made available in the local namespace in one of three ways:

- If the module name is followed by *as*, then the name following *as* is bound directly to the imported module.

- If no other name is specified, and the module being imported is a top level module, the module's name is bound in the local namespace as a reference to the imported module

- If the module being imported is *not* a top level module, then the name of the top level package that contains the module is bound in the local namespace as a reference to the top level package. The imported module must be accessed using its full qualified name rather than directly

The *from* form uses a slightly more complex process:

1. find the module specified in the *from* clause, loading and initializing it if necessary;

2. for each of the identifiers specified in the *import* clauses:

   (a) check if the imported module has an attribute by that name

   (b) if not, attempt to import a submodule with that name and then check the imported module again for that attribute

   (c) if the attribute is not found, ImportError is raised.

   (d) otherwise, a reference to that value is stored in the local namespace, using the name in the *as* clause if it is present, otherwise using the attribute name

Examples:

```
import foo                 # foo imported and bound locally
import foo.bar.baz         # foo.bar.baz imported, foo bound locally
import foo.bar.baz as fbb  # foo.bar.baz imported and bound as fbb
from foo.bar import baz    # foo.bar.baz imported and bound as baz
from foo import attr       # foo imported and foo.attr bound as attr
```

If the list of identifiers is replaced by a star ('*'), all public names defined in the module are bound in the local namespace for the scope where the *import* statement occurs.

The *public names* defined by a module are determined by checking the module's namespace for a variable named __all__; if defined, it must be a sequence of strings which are names defined or imported by that module. The names given in __all__ are all considered public and are required to exist. If __all__ is not defined, the set of public names includes all names found in the module's namespace which do not begin

---

7.11. The import statement

with an underscore character (`'_'`). `__all__` should contain the entire public API. It is intended to avoid accidentally exporting items that are not part of the API (such as library modules which were imported and used within the module).

The wild card form of import — `from module import *` — is only allowed at the module level. Attempting to use it in class or function definitions will raise a `SyntaxError`.

When specifying what module to import you do not have to specify the absolute name of the module. When a module or package is contained within another package it is possible to make a relative import within the same top package without having to mention the package name. By using leading dots in the specified module or package after *from* you can specify how high to traverse up the current package hierarchy without specifying exact names. One leading dot means the current package where the module making the import exists. Two dots means up one package level. Three dots is up two levels, etc. So if you execute `from .` `import mod` from a module in the `pkg` package then you will end up importing `pkg.mod`. If you execute `from ..subpkg2 import mod` from within `pkg.subpkg1` you will import `pkg.subpkg2.mod`. The specification for relative imports is contained within PEP 328.

`importlib.import_module()` is provided to support applications that determine dynamically the modules to be loaded.

7.11.1 Future statements

A *future statement* is a directive to the compiler that a particular module should be compiled using syntax or semantics that will be available in a specified future release of Python where the feature becomes standard.

The future statement is intended to ease migration to future versions of Python that introduce incompatible changes to the language. It allows use of the new features on a per-module basis before the release in which the feature becomes standard.

```
future_statement   ::=    "from" "__future__" "import" feature ["as" name]
                          ("," feature ["as" name])*
                          | "from" "__future__" "import" "(" feature ["as" name]
                          ("," feature ["as" name])* [","] ")"
feature            ::=    identifier
name               ::=    identifier
```

A future statement must appear near the top of the module. The only lines that can appear before a future statement are:

- the module docstring (if any),
- comments,
- blank lines, and
- other future statements.

The features recognized by Python 3.0 are `absolute_import`, `division`, `generators`, `unicode_literals`, `print_function`, `nested_scopes` and `with_statement`. They are all redundant because they are always enabled, and only kept for backwards compatibility.

A future statement is recognized and treated specially at compile time: Changes to the semantics of core constructs are often implemented by generating different code. It may even be the case that a new feature introduces new incompatible syntax (such as a new reserved word), in which case the compiler may need to parse the module differently. Such decisions cannot be pushed off until runtime.

For any given release, the compiler knows which feature names have been defined, and raises a compile-time error if a future statement contains a feature not known to it.

The direct runtime semantics are the same as for any import statement: there is a standard module `__future__`, described later, and it will be imported in the usual way at the time the future statement is executed.

The interesting runtime semantics depend on the specific feature enabled by the future statement.

Note that there is nothing special about the statement:

```
import __future__ [as name]
```

That is not a future statement; it's an ordinary import statement with no special semantics or syntax restrictions.

Code compiled by calls to the built-in functions `exec()` and `compile()` that occur in a module M containing a future statement will, by default, use the new syntax or semantics associated with the future statement. This can be controlled by optional arguments to `compile()` — see the documentation of that function for details.

A future statement typed at an interactive interpreter prompt will take effect for the rest of the interpreter session. If an interpreter is started with the `-i` option, is passed a script name to execute, and the script includes a future statement, it will be in effect in the interactive session started after the script is executed.

See also:

PEP 236 - **Back to the __future__** The original proposal for the __future__ mechanism.

7.12 The global statement

```
global_stmt ::= "global" identifier ("," identifier)*
```

The *global* statement is a declaration which holds for the entire current code block. It means that the listed identifiers are to be interpreted as globals. It would be impossible to assign to a global variable without *global*, although free variables may refer to globals without being declared global.

Names listed in a *global* statement must not be used in the same code block textually preceding that *global* statement.

Names listed in a *global* statement must not be defined as formal parameters or in a *for* loop control target, *class* definition, function definition, *import* statement, or variable annotation.

CPython implementation detail: The current implementation does not enforce some of these restrictions, but programs should not abuse this freedom, as future implementations may enforce them or silently change the meaning of the program.

Programmer's note: *global* is a directive to the parser. It applies only to code parsed at the same time as the *global* statement. In particular, a *global* statement contained in a string or code object supplied to the built-in `exec()` function does not affect the code block *containing* the function call, and code contained in such a string is unaffected by *global* statements in the code containing the function call. The same applies to the `eval()` and `compile()` functions.

7.13 The nonlocal statement

```
nonlocal_stmt ::= "nonlocal" identifier ("," identifier)*
```

The *nonlocal* statement causes the listed identifiers to refer to previously bound variables in the nearest enclosing scope excluding globals. This is important because the default behavior for binding is to search the local namespace first. The statement allows encapsulated code to rebind variables outside of the local scope besides the global (module) scope.

Names listed in a *nonlocal* statement, unlike those listed in a *global* statement, must refer to pre-existing bindings in an enclosing scope (the scope in which a new binding should be created cannot be determined unambiguously).

Names listed in a *nonlocal* statement must not collide with pre-existing bindings in the local scope.

See also:

PEP 3104 - **Access to Names in Outer Scopes** The specification for the *nonlocal* statement.

COMPOUND STATEMENTS

Compound statements contain (groups of) other statements; they affect or control the execution of those other statements in some way. In general, compound statements span multiple lines, although in simple incarnations a whole compound statement may be contained in one line.

The *if*, *while* and *for* statements implement traditional control flow constructs. *try* specifies exception handlers and/or cleanup code for a group of statements, while the *with* statement allows the execution of initialization and finalization code around a block of code. Function and class definitions are also syntactically compound statements.

A compound statement consists of one or more 'clauses.' A clause consists of a header and a 'suite.' The clause headers of a particular compound statement are all at the same indentation level. Each clause header begins with a uniquely identifying keyword and ends with a colon. A suite is a group of statements controlled by a clause. A suite can be one or more semicolon-separated simple statements on the same line as the header, following the header's colon, or it can be one or more indented statements on subsequent lines. Only the latter form of a suite can contain nested compound statements; the following is illegal, mostly because it wouldn't be clear to which *if* clause a following *else* clause would belong:

```
if test1: if test2: print(x)
```

Also note that the semicolon binds tighter than the colon in this context, so that in the following example, either all or none of the **print()** calls are executed:

```
if x < y < z: print(x); print(y); print(z)
```

Summarizing:

```
compound_stmt   ::=   if_stmt
                    | while_stmt
                    | for_stmt
                    | try_stmt
                    | with_stmt
                    | funcdef
                    | classdef
                    | async_with_stmt
                    | async_for_stmt
                    | async_funcdef
suite           ::=   stmt_list NEWLINE | NEWLINE INDENT statement+ DEDENT
statement       ::=   stmt_list NEWLINE | compound_stmt
stmt_list       ::=   simple_stmt (";" simple_stmt)* [";"]
```

Note that statements always end in a **NEWLINE** possibly followed by a **DEDENT**. Also note that optional continuation clauses always begin with a keyword that cannot start a statement, thus there are no ambiguities (the 'dangling *else*' problem is solved in Python by requiring nested *if* statements to be indented).

The formatting of the grammar rules in the following sections places each clause on a separate line for clarity.

8.1 The `if` statement

The *if* statement is used for conditional execution:

```
if_stmt   ::=   "if" expression ":" suite
                ( "elif" expression ":" suite )*
                ["else" ":" suite]
```

It selects exactly one of the suites by evaluating the expressions one by one until one is found to be true (see section *Boolean operations* for the definition of true and false); then that suite is executed (and no other part of the *if* statement is executed or evaluated). If all expressions are false, the suite of the *else* clause, if present, is executed.

8.2 The `while` statement

The *while* statement is used for repeated execution as long as an expression is true:

```
while_stmt   ::=   "while" expression ":" suite
                   ["else" ":" suite]
```

This repeatedly tests the expression and, if it is true, executes the first suite; if the expression is false (which may be the first time it is tested) the suite of the *else* clause, if present, is executed and the loop terminates.

A *break* statement executed in the first suite terminates the loop without executing the *else* clause's suite. A *continue* statement executed in the first suite skips the rest of the suite and goes back to testing the expression.

8.3 The `for` statement

The *for* statement is used to iterate over the elements of a sequence (such as a string, tuple or list) or other iterable object:

```
for_stmt   ::=   "for" target_list "in" expression_list ":" suite
                 ["else" ":" suite]
```

The expression list is evaluated once; it should yield an iterable object. An iterator is created for the result of the **expression_list**. The suite is then executed once for each item provided by the iterator, in the order returned by the iterator. Each item in turn is assigned to the target list using the standard rules for assignments (see *Assignment statements*), and then the suite is executed. When the items are exhausted (which is immediately when the sequence is empty or an iterator raises a `StopIteration` exception), the suite in the *else* clause, if present, is executed, and the loop terminates.

A *break* statement executed in the first suite terminates the loop without executing the *else* clause's suite.

A *continue* statement executed in the first suite skips the rest of the suite and continues with the next item, or with the *else* clause if there is no next item.

The for-loop makes assignments to the variables(s) in the target list. This overwrites all previous assignments to those variables including those made in the suite of the for-loop:

```
for i in range(10):
    print(i)
    i = 5               # this will not affect the for-loop
                        # because i will be overwritten with the next
                        # index in the range
```

Names in the target list are not deleted when the loop is finished, but if the sequence is empty, they will not have been assigned to at all by the loop. Hint: the built-in function **range()** returns an iterator of integers suitable to emulate the effect of Pascal's **for i := a to b do**; e.g., **list(range(3))** returns the list **[0, 1, 2]**.

Note: There is a subtlety when the sequence is being modified by the loop (this can only occur for mutable sequences, i.e. lists). An internal counter is used to keep track of which item is used next, and this is incremented on each iteration. When this counter has reached the length of the sequence the loop terminates. This means that if the suite deletes the current (or a previous) item from the sequence, the next item will be skipped (since it gets the index of the current item which has already been treated). Likewise, if the suite inserts an item in the sequence before the current item, the current item will be treated again the next time through the loop. This can lead to nasty bugs that can be avoided by making a temporary copy using a slice of the whole sequence, e.g.,

```
for x in a[:]:
    if x < 0: a.remove(x)
```

8.4 The `try` statement

The *try* statement specifies exception handlers and/or cleanup code for a group of statements:

```
try_stmt   ::=   try1_stmt | try2_stmt
try1_stmt  ::=   "try" ":" suite
                 ("except" [expression ["as" identifier]] ":" suite)+
                 ["else" ":" suite]
                 ["finally" ":" suite]
try2_stmt  ::=   "try" ":" suite
                 "finally" ":" suite
```

The *except* clause(s) specify one or more exception handlers. When no exception occurs in the *try* clause, no exception handler is executed. When an exception occurs in the *try* suite, a search for an exception handler is started. This search inspects the except clauses in turn until one is found that matches the exception. An expression-less except clause, if present, must be last; it matches any exception. For an except clause with an expression, that expression is evaluated, and the clause matches the exception if the resulting object is "compatible" with the exception. An object is compatible with an exception if it is the class or a base class of the exception object or a tuple containing an item compatible with the exception.

If no except clause matches the exception, the search for an exception handler continues in the surrounding

---

code and on the invocation stack.[1]

If the evaluation of an expression in the header of an except clause raises an exception, the original search for a handler is canceled and a search starts for the new exception in the surrounding code and on the call stack (it is treated as if the entire *try* statement raised the exception).

When a matching except clause is found, the exception is assigned to the target specified after the *as* keyword in that except clause, if present, and the except clause's suite is executed. All except clauses must have an executable block. When the end of this block is reached, execution continues normally after the entire try statement. (This means that if two nested handlers exist for the same exception, and the exception occurs in the try clause of the inner handler, the outer handler will not handle the exception.)

When an exception has been assigned using **as target**, it is cleared at the end of the except clause. This is as if

```
except E as N:
    foo
```

was translated to

```
except E as N:
    try:
        foo
    finally:
        del N
```

This means the exception must be assigned to a different name to be able to refer to it after the except clause. Exceptions are cleared because with the traceback attached to them, they form a reference cycle with the stack frame, keeping all locals in that frame alive until the next garbage collection occurs.

Before an except clause's suite is executed, details about the exception are stored in the **sys** module and can be accessed via **sys.exc_info()**. **sys.exc_info()** returns a 3-tuple consisting of the exception class, the exception instance and a traceback object (see section *The standard type hierarchy*) identifying the point in the program where the exception occurred. **sys.exc_info()** values are restored to their previous values (before the call) when returning from a function that handled an exception.

The optional *else* clause is executed if and when control flows off the end of the *try* clause.[2] Exceptions in the *else* clause are not handled by the preceding *except* clauses.

If *finally* is present, it specifies a 'cleanup' handler. The *try* clause is executed, including any *except* and *else* clauses. If an exception occurs in any of the clauses and is not handled, the exception is temporarily saved. The *finally* clause is executed. If there is a saved exception it is re-raised at the end of the *finally* clause. If the *finally* clause raises another exception, the saved exception is set as the context of the new exception. If the *finally* clause executes a *return* or *break* statement, the saved exception is discarded:

```
>>> def f():
...     try:
...         1/0
...     finally:
...         return 42
...
>>> f()
42
```

The exception information is not available to the program during execution of the *finally* clause.

---

[1] The exception is propagated to the invocation stack unless there is a *finally* clause which happens to raise another exception. That new exception causes the old one to be lost.

[2] Currently, control "flows off the end" except in the case of an exception or the execution of a *return*, *continue*, or *break* statement.

When a *return*, *break* or *continue* statement is executed in the *try* suite of a *try...finally* statement, the *finally* clause is also executed 'on the way out.' A *continue* statement is illegal in the *finally* clause. (The reason is a problem with the current implementation — this restriction may be lifted in the future).

The return value of a function is determined by the last *return* statement executed. Since the *finally* clause always executes, a *return* statement executed in the *finally* clause will always be the last one executed:

```
>>> def foo():
...     try:
...         return 'try'
...     finally:
...         return 'finally'
...
>>> foo()
'finally'
```

Additional information on exceptions can be found in section *Exceptions*, and information on using the *raise* statement to generate exceptions may be found in section *The raise statement*.

8.5 The with statement

The *with* statement is used to wrap the execution of a block with methods defined by a context manager (see section *With Statement Context Managers*). This allows common *try...except...finally* usage patterns to be encapsulated for convenient reuse.

```
with_stmt   ::=   "with" with_item ("," with_item)* ":" suite
with_item   ::=   expression ["as" target]
```

The execution of the *with* statement with one "item" proceeds as follows:

1. The context expression (the expression given in the *with_item*) is evaluated to obtain a context manager.

2. The context manager's __exit__() is loaded for later use.

3. The context manager's __enter__() method is invoked.

4. If a target was included in the *with* statement, the return value from __enter__() is assigned to it.

Note: The *with* statement guarantees that if the __enter__() method returns without an error, then __exit__() will always be called. Thus, if an error occurs during the assignment to the target list, it will be treated the same as an error occurring within the suite would be. See step 6 below.

---

5. The suite is executed.

6. The context manager's __exit__() method is invoked. If an exception caused the suite to be exited, its type, value, and traceback are passed as arguments to __exit__(). Otherwise, three **None** arguments are supplied.

   If the suite was exited due to an exception, and the return value from the __exit__() method was false, the exception is reraised. If the return value was true, the exception is suppressed, and execution continues with the statement following the *with* statement.

   If the suite was exited for any reason other than an exception, the return value from __exit__() is ignored, and execution proceeds at the normal location for the kind of exit that was taken.

With more than one item, the context managers are processed as if multiple *with* statements were nested:

```
with A() as a, B() as b:
    suite
```

is equivalent to

```
with A() as a:
    with B() as b:
        suite
```

Changed in version 3.1: Support for multiple context expressions.

See also:

PEP 343 - **The "with" statement** The specification, background, and examples for the Python *with* statement.

8.6 Function definitions

A function definition defines a user-defined function object (see section *The standard type hierarchy*):

funcdef	::=	[*decorators*] "def" *funcname* "(" [*parameter_list*] ")" ["->" *expression*]
decorators	::=	*decorator+*
decorator	::=	"@" *dotted_name* ["(" [*argument_list* [","]] ")"] NEWLINE
dotted_name	::=	*identifier* ("." *identifier*)*
parameter_list	::=	*defparameter* ("," *defparameter*)* ["," [*parameter_list_starargs*]]
		| *parameter_list_starargs*
parameter_list_starargs	::=	"*" [*parameter*] ("," *defparameter*)* ["," ["**" *parameter* [","]]]
		| "**" *parameter* [","]
parameter	::=	*identifier* [":" *expression*]
defparameter	::=	*parameter* ["=" *expression*]
funcname	::=	*identifier*

A function definition is an executable statement. Its execution binds the function name in the current local namespace to a function object (a wrapper around the executable code for the function). This function object contains a reference to the current global namespace as the global namespace to be used when the function is called.

The function definition does not execute the function body; this gets executed only when the function is called.[3]

A function definition may be wrapped by one or more *decorator* expressions. Decorator expressions are evaluated when the function is defined, in the scope that contains the function definition. The result must be a callable, which is invoked with the function object as the only argument. The returned value is bound to the function name instead of the function object. Multiple decorators are applied in nested fashion. For example, the following code

```
@f1(arg)
@f2
def func(): pass
```

is roughly equivalent to

---

[3] A string literal appearing as the first statement in the function body is transformed into the function's `__doc__` attribute and therefore the function's *docstring*.

```
def func(): pass
func = f1(arg)(f2(func))
```

except that the original function is not temporarily bound to the name func.

When one or more *parameters* have the form *parameter* = *expression*, the function is said to have "default parameter values." For a parameter with a default value, the corresponding *argument* may be omitted from a call, in which case the parameter's default value is substituted. If a parameter has a default value, all following parameters up until the "*" must also have a default value — this is a syntactic restriction that is not expressed by the grammar.

Default parameter values are evaluated from left to right when the function definition is executed. This means that the expression is evaluated once, when the function is defined, and that the same "pre-computed" value is used for each call. This is especially important to understand when a default parameter is a mutable object, such as a list or a dictionary: if the function modifies the object (e.g. by appending an item to a list), the default value is in effect modified. This is generally not what was intended. A way around this is to use None as the default, and explicitly test for it in the body of the function, e.g.:

```
def whats_on_the_telly(penguin=None):
    if penguin is None:
        penguin = []
    penguin.append("property of the zoo")
    return penguin
```

Function call semantics are described in more detail in section *Calls*. A function call always assigns values to all parameters mentioned in the parameter list, either from position arguments, from keyword arguments, or from default values. If the form "*identifier*" is present, it is initialized to a tuple receiving any excess positional parameters, defaulting to the empty tuple. If the form "**identifier*" is present, it is initialized to a new ordered mapping receiving any excess keyword arguments, defaulting to a new empty mapping of the same type. Parameters after "*" or "*identifier*" are keyword-only parameters and may only be passed used keyword arguments.

Parameters may have annotations of the form ": expression" following the parameter name. Any parameter may have an annotation even those of the form *identifier or **identifier. Functions may have "return" annotation of the form "-> expression" after the parameter list. These annotations can be any valid Python expression and are evaluated when the function definition is executed. Annotations may be evaluated in a different order than they appear in the source code. The presence of annotations does not change the semantics of a function. The annotation values are available as values of a dictionary keyed by the parameters' names in the __annotations__ attribute of the function object.

It is also possible to create anonymous functions (functions not bound to a name), for immediate use in expressions. This uses lambda expressions, described in section *Lambdas*. Note that the lambda expression is merely a shorthand for a simplified function definition; a function defined in a "*def*" statement can be passed around or assigned to another name just like a function defined by a lambda expression. The "*def*" form is actually more powerful since it allows the execution of multiple statements and annotations.

Programmer's note: Functions are first-class objects. A "**def**" statement executed inside a function definition defines a local function that can be returned or passed around. Free variables used in the nested function can access the local variables of the function containing the def. See section *Naming and binding* for details.

See also:

PEP 3107 - **Function Annotations** The original specification for function annotations.

8.7 Class definitions

A class definition defines a class object (see section *The standard type hierarchy*):

```
classdef    ::=    [decorators] "class" classname [inheritance] ":" suite
inheritance ::=    "(" [argument_list] ")"
classname   ::=    identifier
```

A class definition is an executable statement. The inheritance list usually gives a list of base classes (see *Metaclasses* for more advanced uses), so each item in the list should evaluate to a class object which allows subclassing. Classes without an inheritance list inherit, by default, from the base class `object`; hence,

```
class Foo:
    pass
```

is equivalent to

```
class Foo(object):
    pass
```

The class's suite is then executed in a new execution frame (see *Naming and binding*), using a newly created local namespace and the original global namespace. (Usually, the suite contains mostly function definitions.) When the class's suite finishes execution, its execution frame is discarded but its local namespace is saved.[4] A class object is then created using the inheritance list for the base classes and the saved local namespace for the attribute dictionary. The class name is bound to this class object in the original local namespace.

The order in which attributes are defined in the class body is preserved in the new class's `__dict__`. Note that this is reliable only right after the class is created and only for classes that were defined using the definition syntax.

Class creation can be customized heavily using *metaclasses*.

Classes can also be decorated: just like when decorating functions,

```
@f1(arg)
@f2
class Foo: pass
```

is roughly equivalent to

```
class Foo: pass
Foo = f1(arg)(f2(Foo))
```

The evaluation rules for the decorator expressions are the same as for function decorators. The result is then bound to the class name.

Programmer's note: Variables defined in the class definition are class attributes; they are shared by instances. Instance attributes can be set in a method with `self.name = value`. Both class and instance attributes are accessible through the notation "`self.name`", and an instance attribute hides a class attribute with the same name when accessed in this way. Class attributes can be used as defaults for instance attributes, but using mutable values there can lead to unexpected results. *Descriptors* can be used to create instance variables with different implementation details.

See also:

PEP 3115 - Metaclasses in Python 3 PEP 3129 - Class Decorators

---

[4] A string literal appearing as the first statement in the class body is transformed into the namespace's `__doc__` item and therefore the class's *docstring*.

8.8 Coroutines

New in version 3.5.

8.8.1 Coroutine function definition

> async_funcdef ::= [*decorators*] "async" "def" *funcname* "(" [*parameter_list*] ")" ["->" *express*

Execution of Python coroutines can be suspended and resumed at many points (see *coroutine*). In the body of a coroutine, any **await** and **async** identifiers become reserved keywords; *await* expressions, *async for* and *async with* can only be used in coroutine bodies.

Functions defined with **async def** syntax are always coroutine functions, even if they do not contain **await** or **async** keywords.

It is a **SyntaxError** to use **yield from** expressions in **async def** coroutines.

An example of a coroutine function:

```
async def func(param1, param2):
    do_stuff()
    await some_coroutine()
```

8.8.2 The async for statement

> async_for_stmt ::= "async" *for_stmt*

An *asynchronous iterable* is able to call asynchronous code in its *iter* implementation, and *asynchronous iterator* can call asynchronous code in its *next* method.

The **async for** statement allows convenient iteration over asynchronous iterators.

The following code:

```
async for TARGET in ITER:
    BLOCK
else:
    BLOCK2
```

Is semantically equivalent to:

```
iter = (ITER)
iter = type(iter).__aiter__(iter)
running = True
while running:
    try:
        TARGET = await type(iter).__anext__(iter)
    except StopAsyncIteration:
        running = False
    else:
        BLOCK
else:
    BLOCK2
```

See also *__aiter__()* and *__anext__()* for details.

It is a **SyntaxError** to use **async for** statement outside of an *async def* function.

8.8.3 The `async with` statement

```
async_with_stmt  ::=    "async" with_stmt
```

An *asynchronous context manager* is a *context manager* that is able to suspend execution in its *enter* and *exit* methods.

The following code:

```
async with EXPR as VAR:
    BLOCK
```

Is semantically equivalent to:

```
mgr = (EXPR)
aexit = type(mgr).__aexit__
aenter = type(mgr).__aenter__(mgr)

VAR = await aenter
try:
    BLOCK
except:
    if not await aexit(mgr, *sys.exc_info()):
        raise
else:
    await aexit(mgr, None, None, None)
```

See also `__aenter__()` and `__aexit__()` for details.

It is a `SyntaxError` to use `async with` statement outside of an *async def* function.

See also:

PEP 492 - Coroutines with async and await syntax

TOP-LEVEL COMPONENTS

The Python interpreter can get its input from a number of sources: from a script passed to it as standard input or as program argument, typed in interactively, from a module source file, etc. This chapter gives the syntax used in these cases.

9.1 Complete Python programs

While a language specification need not prescribe how the language interpreter is invoked, it is useful to have a notion of a complete Python program. A complete Python program is executed in a minimally initialized environment: all built-in and standard modules are available, but none have been initialized, except for `sys` (various system services), `builtins` (built-in functions, exceptions and `None`) and `__main__`. The latter is used to provide the local and global namespace for execution of the complete program.

The syntax for a complete Python program is that for file input, described in the next section.

The interpreter may also be invoked in interactive mode; in this case, it does not read and execute a complete program but reads and executes one statement (possibly compound) at a time. The initial environment is identical to that of a complete program; each statement is executed in the namespace of `__main__`.

Under Unix, a complete program can be passed to the interpreter in three forms: with the `-c` *string* command line option, as a file passed as the first command line argument, or as standard input. If the file or standard input is a tty device, the interpreter enters interactive mode; otherwise, it executes the file as a complete program.

9.2 File input

All input read from non-interactive files has the same form:

```
file_input   ::=   (NEWLINE | statement)*
```

This syntax is used in the following situations:

- when parsing a complete Python program (from a file or from a string);
- when parsing a module;
- when parsing a string passed to the `exec()` function;

9.3 Interactive input

Input in interactive mode is parsed using the following grammar:

```
interactive_input  ::=    [stmt_list] NEWLINE | compound_stmt NEWLINE
```

Note that a (top-level) compound statement must be followed by a blank line in interactive mode; this is needed to help the parser detect the end of the input.

9.4 Expression input

`eval()` is used for expression input. It ignores leading whitespace. The string argument to `eval()` must have the following form:

```
eval_input  ::=    expression_list NEWLINE*
```

FULL GRAMMAR SPECIFICATION

This is the full Python grammar, as it is read by the parser generator and used to parse Python source files:

```
# Grammar for Python

# NOTE WELL: You should also follow all the steps listed at
# https://devguide.python.org/grammar/

# Start symbols for the grammar:
#       single_input is a single interactive statement;
#       file_input is a module or sequence of commands read from an input file;
#       eval_input is the input for the eval() functions.
# NB: compound_stmt in single_input is followed by extra NEWLINE!
single_input: NEWLINE | simple_stmt | compound_stmt NEWLINE
file_input: (NEWLINE | stmt)* ENDMARKER
eval_input: testlist NEWLINE* ENDMARKER

decorator: '@' dotted_name [ '(' [arglist] ')' ] NEWLINE
decorators: decorator+
decorated: decorators (classdef | funcdef | async_funcdef)

async_funcdef: ASYNC funcdef
funcdef: 'def' NAME parameters ['->' test] ':' suite

parameters: '(' [typedargslist] ')'
typedargslist: (tfpdef ['=' test] (',' tfpdef ['=' test])* [',' [
        '*' [tfpdef] (',' tfpdef ['=' test])* [',' ['**' tfpdef [',']]]
     | '**' tfpdef [',']]]
  | '*' [tfpdef] (',' tfpdef ['=' test])* [',' ['**' tfpdef [',']]]
  | '**' tfpdef [','])
tfpdef: NAME [':' test]
varargslist: (vfpdef ['=' test] (',' vfpdef ['=' test])* [',' [
        '*' [vfpdef] (',' vfpdef ['=' test])* [',' ['**' vfpdef [',']]]
     | '**' vfpdef [',']]]
  | '*' [vfpdef] (',' vfpdef ['=' test])* [',' ['**' vfpdef [',']]]
  | '**' vfpdef [',']
)
vfpdef: NAME

stmt: simple_stmt | compound_stmt
simple_stmt: small_stmt (';' small_stmt)* [';'] NEWLINE
small_stmt: (expr_stmt | del_stmt | pass_stmt | flow_stmt |
             import_stmt | global_stmt | nonlocal_stmt | assert_stmt)
expr_stmt: testlist_star_expr (annassign | augassign (yield_expr|testlist) |
                   ('=' (yield_expr|testlist_star_expr))*)
annassign: ':' test ['=' test]
```

```
testlist_star_expr: (test|star_expr) (',' (test|star_expr))* [',']
augassign: ('+=' | '-=' | '*=' | '@=' | '/=' | '%=' | '&=' | '|=' | '^=' |
            '<<=' | '>>=' | '**=' | '//=')
# For normal and annotated assignments, additional restrictions enforced by the interpreter
del_stmt: 'del' exprlist
pass_stmt: 'pass'
flow_stmt: break_stmt | continue_stmt | return_stmt | raise_stmt | yield_stmt
break_stmt: 'break'
continue_stmt: 'continue'
return_stmt: 'return' [testlist]
yield_stmt: yield_expr
raise_stmt: 'raise' [test ['from' test]]
import_stmt: import_name | import_from
import_name: 'import' dotted_as_names
# note below: the ('.' | '...') is necessary because '...' is tokenized as ELLIPSIS
import_from: ('from' (('.' | '...')* dotted_name | ('.' | '...')+)
              'import' ('*' | '(' import_as_names ')' | import_as_names))
import_as_name: NAME ['as' NAME]
dotted_as_name: dotted_name ['as' NAME]
import_as_names: import_as_name (',' import_as_name)* [',']
dotted_as_names: dotted_as_name (',' dotted_as_name)*
dotted_name: NAME ('.' NAME)*
global_stmt: 'global' NAME (',' NAME)*
nonlocal_stmt: 'nonlocal' NAME (',' NAME)*
assert_stmt: 'assert' test [',' test]

compound_stmt: if_stmt | while_stmt | for_stmt | try_stmt | with_stmt | funcdef | classdef |
   decorated | async_stmt
async_stmt: ASYNC (funcdef | with_stmt | for_stmt)
if_stmt: 'if' test ':' suite ('elif' test ':' suite)* ['else' ':' suite]
while_stmt: 'while' test ':' suite ['else' ':' suite]
for_stmt: 'for' exprlist 'in' testlist ':' suite ['else' ':' suite]
try_stmt: ('try' ':' suite
           ((except_clause ':' suite)+
            ['else' ':' suite]
            ['finally' ':' suite] |
            'finally' ':' suite))
with_stmt: 'with' with_item (',' with_item)*  ':' suite
with_item: test ['as' expr]
# NB compile.c makes sure that the default except clause is last
except_clause: 'except' [test ['as' NAME]]
suite: simple_stmt | NEWLINE INDENT stmt+ DEDENT

test: or_test ['if' or_test 'else' test] | lambdef
test_nocond: or_test | lambdef_nocond
lambdef: 'lambda' [varargslist] ':' test
lambdef_nocond: 'lambda' [varargslist] ':' test_nocond
or_test: and_test ('or' and_test)*
and_test: not_test ('and' not_test)*
not_test: 'not' not_test | comparison
comparison: expr (comp_op expr)*
# <> isn't actually a valid comparison operator in Python. It's here for the
# sake of a __future__ import described in PEP 401 (which really works :-)
comp_op: '<'|'>'|'=='|'>='|'<='|'<>'|'!='|'in'|'not' 'in'|'is'|'is' 'not'
star_expr: '*' expr
expr: xor_expr ('|' xor_expr)*
xor_expr: and_expr ('^' and_expr)*
and_expr: shift_expr ('&' shift_expr)*
```

```
shift_expr: arith_expr (('<<'|'>>') arith_expr)*
arith_expr: term (('+'|'-') term)*
term: factor (('*'|'@'|'/'|'%'|'//') factor)*
factor: ('+'|'-'|'~') factor | power
power: atom_expr ['**' factor]
atom_expr: [AWAIT] atom trailer*
atom: ('(' [yield_expr|testlist_comp] ')' |
       '[' [testlist_comp] ']' |
       '{' [dictorsetmaker] '}' |
       NAME | NUMBER | STRING+ | '...' | 'None' | 'True' | 'False')
testlist_comp: (test|star_expr) ( comp_for | (',' (test|star_expr))* [','] )
trailer: '(' [arglist] ')' | '[' subscriptlist ']' | '.' NAME
subscriptlist: subscript (',' subscript)* [',']
subscript: test | [test] ':' [test] [sliceop]
sliceop: ':' [test]
exprlist: (expr|star_expr) (',' (expr|star_expr))* [',']
testlist: test (',' test)* [',']
dictorsetmaker: ( ((test ':' test | '**' expr)
                   (comp_for | (',' (test ':' test | '**' expr))* [','])) |
                  ((test | star_expr)
                   (comp_for | (',' (test | star_expr))* [','])) )

classdef: 'class' NAME ['(' [arglist] ')'] ':' suite

arglist: argument (',' argument)*  [',']

# The reason that keywords are test nodes instead of NAME is that using NAME
# results in an ambiguity. ast.c makes sure it's a NAME.
# "test '=' test" is really "keyword '=' test", but we have no such token.
# These need to be in a single rule to avoid grammar that is ambiguous
# to our LL(1) parser. Even though 'test' includes '*expr' in star_expr,
# we explicitly match '*' here, too, to give it proper precedence.
# Illegal combinations and orderings are blocked in ast.c:
# multiple (test comp_for) arguments are blocked; keyword unpackings
# that precede iterable unpackings are blocked; etc.
argument: ( test [comp_for] |
            test '=' test |
            '**' test |
            '*' test )

comp_iter: comp_for | comp_if
comp_for: [ASYNC] 'for' exprlist 'in' or_test [comp_iter]
comp_if: 'if' test_nocond [comp_iter]

# not used in grammar, but may appear in "node" passed from Parser to Compiler
encoding_decl: NAME

yield_expr: 'yield' [yield_arg]
yield_arg: 'from' test | testlist
```

GLOSSARY

>>> The default Python prompt of the interactive shell. Often seen for code examples which can be executed interactively in the interpreter.

... The default Python prompt of the interactive shell when entering code for an indented code block or within a pair of matching left and right delimiters (parentheses, square brackets or curly braces).

2to3 A tool that tries to convert Python 2.x code to Python 3.x code by handling most of the incompatibilities which can be detected by parsing the source and traversing the parse tree.

> 2to3 is available in the standard library as `lib2to3`; a standalone entry point is provided as `Tools/scripts/2to3`. See 2to3-reference.

abstract base class Abstract base classes complement *duck-typing* by providing a way to define interfaces when other techniques like `hasattr()` would be clumsy or subtly wrong (for example with *magic methods*). ABCs introduce virtual subclasses, which are classes that don't inherit from a class but are still recognized by `isinstance()` and `issubclass()`; see the `abc` module documentation. Python comes with many built-in ABCs for data structures (in the `collections.abc` module), numbers (in the `numbers` module), streams (in the `io` module), import finders and loaders (in the `importlib.abc` module). You can create your own ABCs with the `abc` module.

argument A value passed to a *function* (or *method*) when calling the function. There are two kinds of argument:

- *keyword argument*: an argument preceded by an identifier (e.g. `name=`) in a function call or passed as a value in a dictionary preceded by `**`. For example, 3 and 5 are both keyword arguments in the following calls to `complex()`:

```
complex(real=3, imag=5)
complex(**{'real': 3, 'imag': 5})
```

- *positional argument*: an argument that is not a keyword argument. Positional arguments can appear at the beginning of an argument list and/or be passed as elements of an *iterable* preceded by `*`. For example, 3 and 5 are both positional arguments in the following calls:

```
complex(3, 5)
complex(*(3, 5))
```

Arguments are assigned to the named local variables in a function body. See the *Calls* section for the rules governing this assignment. Syntactically, any expression can be used to represent an argument; the evaluated value is assigned to the local variable.

See also the *parameter* glossary entry, the FAQ question on the difference between arguments and parameters, and PEP 362.

asynchronous context manager An object which controls the environment seen in an *async with* statement by defining `__aenter__()` and `__aexit__()` methods. Introduced by PEP 492.

asynchronous generator A function which returns an *asynchronous generator iterator*. It looks like a coroutine function defined with `async def` except that it contains `yield` expressions for producing a series of values usable in an `async for` loop.

Usually refers to a asynchronous generator function, but may refer to an *asynchronous generator iterator* in some contexts. In cases where the intended meaning isn't clear, using the full terms avoids ambiguity.

An asynchronous generator function may contain `await` expressions as well as `async for`, and `async with` statements.

asynchronous generator iterator An object created by a *asynchronous generator* function.

This is an *asynchronous iterator* which when called using the `__anext__ ()` method returns an awaitable object which will execute that the body of the asynchronous generator function until the next `yield` expression.

Each `yield` temporarily suspends processing, remembering the location execution state (including local variables and pending try-statements). When the *asynchronous generator iterator* effectively resumes with another awaitable returned by `__anext__ ()`, it picks-up where it left-off. See PEP 492 and PEP 525.

asynchronous iterable An object, that can be used in an `async for` statement. Must return an *asynchronous iterator* from its `__aiter__ ()` method. Introduced by PEP 492.

asynchronous iterator An object that implements `__aiter__ ()` and `__anext__ ()` methods. `__anext__` must return an *awaitable* object. `async for` resolves awaitable returned from asynchronous iterator's `__anext__ ()` method until it raises `StopAsyncIteration` exception. Introduced by PEP 492.

attribute A value associated with an object which is referenced by name using dotted expressions. For example, if an object *o* has an attribute *a* it would be referenced as *o.a*.

awaitable An object that can be used in an `await` expression. Can be a *coroutine* or an object with an `__await__ ()` method. See also PEP 492.

BDFL Benevolent Dictator For Life, a.k.a. Guido van Rossum, Python's creator.

binary file A *file object* able to read and write *bytes-like objects*. Examples of binary files are files opened in binary mode (`'rb'`, `'wb'` or `'rb+'`), `sys.stdin.buffer`, `sys.stdout.buffer`, and instances of `io.BytesIO` and `gzip.GzipFile`.

See also:

A *text file* reads and writes `str` objects.

bytes-like object An object that supports the bufferobjects and can export a C-*contiguous* buffer. This includes all `bytes`, `bytearray`, and `array.array` objects, as well as many common `memoryview` objects. Bytes-like objects can be used for various operations that work with binary data; these include compression, saving to a binary file, and sending over a socket.

Some operations need the binary data to be mutable. The documentation often refers to these as "read-write bytes-like objects". Example mutable buffer objects include `bytearray` and a `memoryview` of a `bytearray`. Other operations require the binary data to be stored in immutable objects ("read-only bytes-like objects"); examples of these include `bytes` and a `memoryview` of a `bytes` object.

bytecode Python source code is compiled into bytecode, the internal representation of a Python program in the CPython interpreter. The bytecode is also cached in `.pyc` files so that executing the same file is faster the second time (recompilation from source to bytecode can be avoided). This "intermediate language" is said to run on a *virtual machine* that executes the machine code corresponding to each bytecode. Do note that bytecodes are not expected to work between different Python virtual machines, nor to be stable between Python releases.

A list of bytecode instructions can be found in the documentation for the dis module.

class A template for creating user-defined objects. Class definitions normally contain method definitions which operate on instances of the class.

coercion The implicit conversion of an instance of one type to another during an operation which involves two arguments of the same type. For example, `int(3.15)` converts the floating point number to the integer 3, but in 3+4.5, each argument is of a different type (one int, one float), and both must be converted to the same type before they can be added or it will raise a `TypeError`. Without coercion, all arguments of even compatible types would have to be normalized to the same value by the programmer, e.g., `float(3)+4.5` rather than just 3+4.5.

complex number An extension of the familiar real number system in which all numbers are expressed as a sum of a real part and an imaginary part. Imaginary numbers are real multiples of the imaginary unit (the square root of -1), often written i in mathematics or j in engineering. Python has built-in support for complex numbers, which are written with this latter notation; the imaginary part is written with a j suffix, e.g., 3+1j. To get access to complex equivalents of the `math` module, use `cmath`. Use of complex numbers is a fairly advanced mathematical feature. If you're not aware of a need for them, it's almost certain you can safely ignore them.

context manager An object which controls the environment seen in a *with* statement by defining *__enter__* () and *__exit__* () methods. See PEP 343.

contiguous A buffer is considered contiguous exactly if it is either *C-contiguous* or *Fortran contiguous*. Zero-dimensional buffers are C and Fortran contiguous. In one-dimensional arrays, the items must be laid out in memory next to each other, in order of increasing indexes starting from zero. In multidimensional C-contiguous arrays, the last index varies the fastest when visiting items in order of memory address. However, in Fortran contiguous arrays, the first index varies the fastest.

coroutine Coroutines is a more generalized form of subroutines. Subroutines are entered at one point and exited at another point. Coroutines can be entered, exited, and resumed at many different points. They can be implemented with the *async def* statement. See also PEP 492.

coroutine function A function which returns a *coroutine* object. A coroutine function may be defined with the *async def* statement, and may contain *await*, *async for*, and *async with* keywords. These were introduced by PEP 492.

CPython The canonical implementation of the Python programming language, as distributed on python.org. The term "CPython" is used when necessary to distinguish this implementation from others such as Jython or IronPython.

decorator A function returning another function, usually applied as a function transformation using the `@wrapper` syntax. Common examples for decorators are `classmethod()` and `staticmethod()`.

The decorator syntax is merely syntactic sugar, the following two function definitions are semantically equivalent:

```
def f(...):
    ...
f = staticmethod(f)

@staticmethod
def f(...):
    ...
```

The same concept exists for classes, but is less commonly used there. See the documentation for *function definitions* and *class definitions* for more about decorators.

descriptor Any object which defines the methods *__get__* (), *__set__* (), or *__delete__* (). When a class attribute is a descriptor, its special binding behavior is triggered upon attribute lookup. Normally, using *a.b* to get, set or delete an attribute looks up the object named *b* in the class dictionary for *a*, but if *b* is a descriptor, the respective descriptor method gets called. Understanding descriptors is a key to a deep understanding of Python because they are the basis for many features including functions, methods, properties, class methods, static methods, and reference to super classes.

For more information about descriptors' methods, see *Implementing Descriptors*.

dictionary An associative array, where arbitrary keys are mapped to values. The keys can be any object with `__hash__()` and `__eq__()` methods. Called a hash in Perl.

dictionary view The objects returned from `dict.keys()`, `dict.values()`, and `dict.items()` are called dictionary views. They provide a dynamic view on the dictionary's entries, which means that when the dictionary changes, the view reflects these changes. To force the dictionary view to become a full list use `list(dictview)`. See dict-views.

docstring A string literal which appears as the first expression in a class, function or module. While ignored when the suite is executed, it is recognized by the compiler and put into the `__doc__` attribute of the enclosing class, function or module. Since it is available via introspection, it is the canonical place for documentation of the object.

duck-typing A programming style which does not look at an object's type to determine if it has the right interface; instead, the method or attribute is simply called or used ("If it looks like a duck and quacks like a duck, it must be a duck.") By emphasizing interfaces rather than specific types, well-designed code improves its flexibility by allowing polymorphic substitution. Duck-typing avoids tests using `type()` or `isinstance()`. (Note, however, that duck-typing can be complemented with *abstract base classes*.) Instead, it typically employs `hasattr()` tests or *EAFP* programming.

EAFP Easier to ask for forgiveness than permission. This common Python coding style assumes the existence of valid keys or attributes and catches exceptions if the assumption proves false. This clean and fast style is characterized by the presence of many *try* and *except* statements. The technique contrasts with the *LBYL* style common to many other languages such as C.

expression A piece of syntax which can be evaluated to some value. In other words, an expression is an accumulation of expression elements like literals, names, attribute access, operators or function calls which all return a value. In contrast to many other languages, not all language constructs are expressions. There are also *statement*s which cannot be used as expressions, such as *if*. Assignments are also statements, not expressions.

extension module A module written in C or C++, using Python's C API to interact with the core and with user code.

f-string String literals prefixed with `'f'` or `'F'` are commonly called "f-strings" which is short for *formatted string literals*. See also PEP 498.

file object An object exposing a file-oriented API (with methods such as `read()` or `write()`) to an underlying resource. Depending on the way it was created, a file object can mediate access to a real on-disk file or to another type of storage or communication device (for example standard input/output, in-memory buffers, sockets, pipes, etc.). File objects are also called *file-like objects* or *streams*.

There are actually three categories of file objects: raw *binary files*, buffered *binary files* and *text files*. Their interfaces are defined in the `io` module. The canonical way to create a file object is by using the `open()` function.

file-like object A synonym for *file object*.

finder An object that tries to find the *loader* for a module that is being imported.

Since Python 3.3, there are two types of finder: *meta path finders* for use with `sys.meta_path`, and *path entry finders* for use with `sys.path_hooks`.

See PEP 302, PEP 420 and PEP 451 for much more detail.

floor division Mathematical division that rounds down to nearest integer. The floor division operator is `//`. For example, the expression `11 // 4` evaluates to `2` in contrast to the `2.75` returned by float true division. Note that `(-11) // 4` is `-3` because that is `-2.75` rounded *downward*. See PEP 238.

function A series of statements which returns some value to a caller. It can also be passed zero or more *arguments* which may be used in the execution of the body. See also *parameter*, *method*, and the *Function definitions* section.

function annotation An arbitrary metadata value associated with a function parameter or return value. Its syntax is explained in section *Function definitions*. Annotations may be accessed via the `__annotations__` special attribute of a function object.

Python itself does not assign any particular meaning to function annotations. They are intended to be interpreted by third-party libraries or tools. See PEP 3107, which describes some of their potential uses.

__future__ A pseudo-module which programmers can use to enable new language features which are not compatible with the current interpreter.

By importing the `__future__` module and evaluating its variables, you can see when a new feature was first added to the language and when it becomes the default:

```
>>> import __future__
>>> __future__.division
_Feature((2, 2, 0, 'alpha', 2), (3, 0, 0, 'alpha', 0), 8192)
```

garbage collection The process of freeing memory when it is not used anymore. Python performs garbage collection via reference counting and a cyclic garbage collector that is able to detect and break reference cycles. The garbage collector can be controlled using the `gc` module.

generator A function which returns a *generator iterator*. It looks like a normal function except that it contains `yield` expressions for producing a series of values usable in a for-loop or that can be retrieved one at a time with the `next()` function.

Usually refers to a generator function, but may refer to a *generator iterator* in some contexts. In cases where the intended meaning isn't clear, using the full terms avoids ambiguity.

generator iterator An object created by a *generator* function.

Each `yield` temporarily suspends processing, remembering the location execution state (including local variables and pending try-statements). When the *generator iterator* resumes, it picks-up where it left-off (in contrast to functions which start fresh on every invocation).

generator expression An expression that returns an iterator. It looks like a normal expression followed by a `for` expression defining a loop variable, range, and an optional `if` expression. The combined expression generates values for an enclosing function:

```
>>> sum(i*i for i in range(10))         # sum of squares 0, 1, 4, ... 81
285
```

generic function A function composed of multiple functions implementing the same operation for different types. Which implementation should be used during a call is determined by the dispatch algorithm.

See also the *single dispatch* glossary entry, the `functools.singledispatch()` decorator, and PEP 443.

GIL See *global interpreter lock*.

global interpreter lock The mechanism used by the *CPython* interpreter to assure that only one thread executes Python *bytecode* at a time. This simplifies the CPython implementation by making the object model (including critical built-in types such as `dict`) implicitly safe against concurrent access. Locking the entire interpreter makes it easier for the interpreter to be multi-threaded, at the expense of much of the parallelism afforded by multi-processor machines.

However, some extension modules, either standard or third-party, are designed so as to release the GIL when doing computationally-intensive tasks such as compression or hashing. Also, the GIL is always released when doing I/O.

Past efforts to create a "free-threaded" interpreter (one which locks shared data at a much finer granularity) have not been successful because performance suffered in the common single-processor case. It is believed that overcoming this performance issue would make the implementation much more complicated and therefore costlier to maintain.

hashable An object is *hashable* if it has a hash value which never changes during its lifetime (it needs a `__hash__()` method), and can be compared to other objects (it needs an `__eq__()` method). Hashable objects which compare equal must have the same hash value.

Hashability makes an object usable as a dictionary key and a set member, because these data structures use the hash value internally.

All of Python's immutable built-in objects are hashable; mutable containers (such as lists or dictionaries) are not. Objects which are instances of user-defined classes are hashable by default. They all compare unequal (except with themselves), and their hash value is derived from their `id()`.

IDLE An Integrated Development Environment for Python. IDLE is a basic editor and interpreter environment which ships with the standard distribution of Python.

immutable An object with a fixed value. Immutable objects include numbers, strings and tuples. Such an object cannot be altered. A new object has to be created if a different value has to be stored. They play an important role in places where a constant hash value is needed, for example as a key in a dictionary.

import path A list of locations (or *path entries*) that are searched by the *path based finder* for modules to import. During import, this list of locations usually comes from `sys.path`, but for subpackages it may also come from the parent package's `__path__` attribute.

importing The process by which Python code in one module is made available to Python code in another module.

importer An object that both finds and loads a module; both a *finder* and *loader* object.

interactive Python has an interactive interpreter which means you can enter statements and expressions at the interpreter prompt, immediately execute them and see their results. Just launch **python** with no arguments (possibly by selecting it from your computer's main menu). It is a very powerful way to test out new ideas or inspect modules and packages (remember `help(x)`).

interpreted Python is an interpreted language, as opposed to a compiled one, though the distinction can be blurry because of the presence of the bytecode compiler. This means that source files can be run directly without explicitly creating an executable which is then run. Interpreted languages typically have a shorter development/debug cycle than compiled ones, though their programs generally also run more slowly. See also *interactive*.

interpreter shutdown When asked to shut down, the Python interpreter enters a special phase where it gradually releases all allocated resources, such as modules and various critical internal structures. It also makes several calls to the *garbage collector*. This can trigger the execution of code in user-defined destructors or weakref callbacks. Code executed during the shutdown phase can encounter various exceptions as the resources it relies on may not function anymore (common examples are library modules or the warnings machinery).

The main reason for interpreter shutdown is that the `__main__` module or the script being run has finished executing.

iterable An object capable of returning its members one at a time. Examples of iterables include all sequence types (such as `list`, `str`, and `tuple`) and some non-sequence types like `dict`, *file objects*, and objects of any classes you define with an `__iter__()` method or with a `__getitem__()` method that implements *Sequence* semantics.

Iterables can be used in a *for* loop and in many other places where a sequence is needed (`zip()`, `map()`, ...). When an iterable object is passed as an argument to the built-in function `iter()`, it returns an iterator for the object. This iterator is good for one pass over the set of values. When using iterables, it is usually not necessary to call `iter()` or deal with iterator objects yourself. The `for` statement does that automatically for you, creating a temporary unnamed variable to hold the iterator for the duration of the loop. See also *iterator*, *sequence*, and *generator*.

iterator An object representing a stream of data. Repeated calls to the iterator's `__next__()` method (or passing it to the built-in function `next()`) return successive items in the stream. When no more data are available a `StopIteration` exception is raised instead. At this point, the iterator object is exhausted and any further calls to its `__next__()` method just raise `StopIteration` again. Iterators are required to have an `__iter__()` method that returns the iterator object itself so every iterator is also iterable and may be used in most places where other iterables are accepted. One notable exception is code which attempts multiple iteration passes. A container object (such as a `list`) produces a fresh new iterator each time you pass it to the `iter()` function or use it in a *for* loop. Attempting this with an iterator will just return the same exhausted iterator object used in the previous iteration pass, making it appear like an empty container.

More information can be found in typeiter.

key function A key function or collation function is a callable that returns a value used for sorting or ordering. For example, `locale.strxfrm()` is used to produce a sort key that is aware of locale specific sort conventions.

A number of tools in Python accept key functions to control how elements are ordered or grouped. They include `min()`, `max()`, `sorted()`, `list.sort()`, `heapq.merge()`, `heapq.nsmallest()`, `heapq.nlargest()`, and `itertools.groupby()`.

There are several ways to create a key function. For example. the `str.lower()` method can serve as a key function for case insensitive sorts. Alternatively, a key function can be built from a *lambda* expression such as `lambda r: (r[0], r[2])`. Also, the `operator` module provides three key function constructors: `attrgetter()`, `itemgetter()`, and `methodcaller()`. See the Sorting HOW TO for examples of how to create and use key functions.

keyword argument See *argument*.

lambda An anonymous inline function consisting of a single *expression* which is evaluated when the function is called. The syntax to create a lambda function is `lambda [arguments]: expression`

LBYL Look before you leap. This coding style explicitly tests for pre-conditions before making calls or lookups. This style contrasts with the *EAFP* approach and is characterized by the presence of many *if* statements.

In a multi-threaded environment, the LBYL approach can risk introducing a race condition between "the looking" and "the leaping". For example, the code, `if key in mapping: return mapping[key]` can fail if another thread removes *key* from *mapping* after the test, but before the lookup. This issue can be solved with locks or by using the EAFP approach.

list A built-in Python *sequence*. Despite its name it is more akin to an array in other languages than to a linked list since access to elements are O(1).

list comprehension A compact way to process all or part of the elements in a sequence and return a list with the results. `result = ['{:#04x}'.format(x) for x in range(256) if x % 2 == 0]` generates a list of strings containing even hex numbers (0x..) in the range from 0 to 255. The *if* clause is optional. If omitted, all elements in `range(256)` are processed.

loader An object that loads a module. It must define a method named `load_module()`. A loader is typically returned by a *finder*. See PEP 302 for details and `importlib.abc.Loader` for an *abstract base class*.

mapping A container object that supports arbitrary key lookups and implements the methods specified in the `Mapping` or `MutableMapping` abstract base classes. Examples include `dict`, `collections.defaultdict`, `collections.OrderedDict` and `collections.Counter`.

meta path finder A *finder* returned by a search of `sys.meta_path`. Meta path finders are related to, but different from *path entry finders*.

See `importlib.abc.MetaPathFinder` for the methods that meta path finders implement.

metaclass The class of a class. Class definitions create a class name, a class dictionary, and a list of base classes. The metaclass is responsible for taking those three arguments and creating the class. Most object oriented programming languages provide a default implementation. What makes Python special is that it is possible to create custom metaclasses. Most users never need this tool, but when the need arises, metaclasses can provide powerful, elegant solutions. They have been used for logging attribute access, adding thread-safety, tracking object creation, implementing singletons, and many other tasks.

More information can be found in *Metaclasses*.

method A function which is defined inside a class body. If called as an attribute of an instance of that class, the method will get the instance object as its first *argument* (which is usually called `self`). See *function* and *nested scope*.

method resolution order Method Resolution Order is the order in which base classes are searched for a member during lookup. See The Python 2.3 Method Resolution Order for details of the algorithm used by the Python interpreter since the 2.3 release.

module An object that serves as an organizational unit of Python code. Modules have a namespace containing arbitrary Python objects. Modules are loaded into Python by the process of *importing*.

See also *package*.

module spec A namespace containing the import-related information used to load a module. An instance of `importlib.machinery.ModuleSpec`.

MRO See *method resolution order*.

mutable Mutable objects can change their value but keep their `id()`. See also *immutable*.

named tuple Any tuple-like class whose indexable elements are also accessible using named attributes (for example, `time.localtime()` returns a tuple-like object where the *year* is accessible either with an index such as `t[0]` or with a named attribute like `t.tm_year`).

A named tuple can be a built-in type such as `time.struct_time`, or it can be created with a regular class definition. A full featured named tuple can also be created with the factory function `collections.namedtuple()`. The latter approach automatically provides extra features such as a self-documenting representation like `Employee(name='jones', title='programmer')`.

namespace The place where a variable is stored. Namespaces are implemented as dictionaries. There are the local, global and built-in namespaces as well as nested namespaces in objects (in methods). Namespaces support modularity by preventing naming conflicts. For instance, the functions `builtins.open` and `os.open()` are distinguished by their namespaces. Namespaces also aid readability and maintainability by making it clear which module implements a function. For instance, writing `random.seed()` or `itertools.islice()` makes it clear that those functions are implemented by the `random` and `itertools` modules, respectively.

namespace package A PEP 420 *package* which serves only as a container for subpackages. Namespace packages may have no physical representation, and specifically are not like a *regular package* because they have no `__init__.py` file.

See also *module*.

nested scope The ability to refer to a variable in an enclosing definition. For instance, a function defined inside another function can refer to variables in the outer function. Note that nested scopes by default work only for reference and not for assignment. Local variables both read and write in the innermost scope. Likewise, global variables read and write to the global namespace. The *nonlocal* allows writing to outer scopes.

new-style class Old name for the flavor of classes now used for all class objects. In earlier Python versions, only new-style classes could use Python's newer, versatile features like `__slots__`, descriptors, properties, `__getattribute__()`, class methods, and static methods.

object Any data with state (attributes or value) and defined behavior (methods). Also the ultimate base class of any *new-style class*.

package A Python *module* which can contain submodules or recursively, subpackages. Technically, a package is a Python module with an `__path__` attribute.

See also *regular package* and *namespace package*.

parameter A named entity in a *function* (or method) definition that specifies an *argument* (or in some cases, arguments) that the function can accept. There are five kinds of parameter:

- *positional-or-keyword*: specifies an argument that can be passed either *positionally* or as a *keyword argument*. This is the default kind of parameter, for example *foo* and *bar* in the following:

```
def func(foo, bar=None): ...
```

- *positional-only*: specifies an argument that can be supplied only by position. Python has no syntax for defining positional-only parameters. However, some built-in functions have positional-only parameters (e.g. `abs()`).

- *keyword-only*: specifies an argument that can be supplied only by keyword. Keyword-only parameters can be defined by including a single var-positional parameter or bare `*` in the parameter list of the function definition before them, for example *kw_only1* and *kw_only2* in the following:

```
def func(arg, *, kw_only1, kw_only2): ...
```

- *var-positional*: specifies that an arbitrary sequence of positional arguments can be provided (in addition to any positional arguments already accepted by other parameters). Such a parameter can be defined by prepending the parameter name with `*`, for example *args* in the following:

```
def func(*args, **kwargs): ...
```

- *var-keyword*: specifies that arbitrarily many keyword arguments can be provided (in addition to any keyword arguments already accepted by other parameters). Such a parameter can be defined by prepending the parameter name with `**`, for example *kwargs* in the example above.

Parameters can specify both optional and required arguments, as well as default values for some optional arguments.

See also the *argument* glossary entry, the FAQ question on the difference between arguments and parameters, the `inspect.Parameter` class, the *Function definitions* section, and PEP 362.

path entry A single location on the *import path* which the *path based finder* consults to find modules for importing.

path entry finder A *finder* returned by a callable on `sys.path_hooks` (i.e. a *path entry hook*) which knows how to locate modules given a *path entry*.

See `importlib.abc.PathEntryFinder` for the methods that path entry finders implement.

path entry hook A callable on the `sys.path_hook` list which returns a *path entry finder* if it knows how to find modules on a specific *path entry*.

path based finder One of the default *meta path finders* which searches an *import path* for modules.

path-like object An object representing a file system path. A path-like object is either a `str` or `bytes` object representing a path, or an object implementing the `os.PathLike` protocol. An object that supports the `os.PathLike` protocol can be converted to a `str` or `bytes` file system path by calling the `os.fspath()` function; `os.fsdecode()` and `os.fsencode()` can be used to guarantee a `str` or `bytes` result instead, respectively. Introduced by PEP 519.

portion A set of files in a single directory (possibly stored in a zip file) that contribute to a namespace package, as defined in PEP 420.

positional argument See *argument*.

provisional API A provisional API is one which has been deliberately excluded from the standard library's backwards compatibility guarantees. While major changes to such interfaces are not expected, as long as they are marked provisional, backwards incompatible changes (up to and including removal of the interface) may occur if deemed necessary by core developers. Such changes will not be made gratuitously – they will occur only if serious fundamental flaws are uncovered that were missed prior to the inclusion of the API.

Even for provisional APIs, backwards incompatible changes are seen as a "solution of last resort" - every attempt will still be made to find a backwards compatible resolution to any identified problems.

This process allows the standard library to continue to evolve over time, without locking in problematic design errors for extended periods of time. See PEP 411 for more details.

provisional package See *provisional API*.

Python 3000 Nickname for the Python 3.x release line (coined long ago when the release of version 3 was something in the distant future.) This is also abbreviated "Py3k".

Pythonic An idea or piece of code which closely follows the most common idioms of the Python language, rather than implementing code using concepts common to other languages. For example, a common idiom in Python is to loop over all elements of an iterable using a *for* statement. Many other languages don't have this type of construct, so people unfamiliar with Python sometimes use a numerical counter instead:

```
for i in range(len(food)):
    print(food[i])
```

As opposed to the cleaner, Pythonic method:

```
for piece in food:
    print(piece)
```

qualified name A dotted name showing the "path" from a module's global scope to a class, function or method defined in that module, as defined in PEP 3155. For top-level functions and classes, the qualified name is the same as the object's name:

```
>>> class C:
...     class D:
...         def meth(self):
...             pass
...
>>> C.__qualname__
'C'
>>> C.D.__qualname__
'C.D'
>>> C.D.meth.__qualname__
'C.D.meth'
```

When used to refer to modules, the *fully qualified name* means the entire dotted path to the module, including any parent packages, e.g. `email.mime.text`:

```
>>> import email.mime.text
>>> email.mime.text.__name__
'email.mime.text'
```

reference count The number of references to an object. When the reference count of an object drops to zero, it is deallocated. Reference counting is generally not visible to Python code, but it is a key element of the *CPython* implementation. The sys module defines a getrefcount() function that programmers can call to return the reference count for a particular object.

regular package A traditional *package*, such as a directory containing an __init__.py file.

See also *namespace package*.

__slots__ A declaration inside a class that saves memory by pre-declaring space for instance attributes and eliminating instance dictionaries. Though popular, the technique is somewhat tricky to get right and is best reserved for rare cases where there are large numbers of instances in a memory-critical application.

sequence An *iterable* which supports efficient element access using integer indices via the __getitem__() special method and defines a __len__() method that returns the length of the sequence. Some built-in sequence types are list, str, tuple, and bytes. Note that dict also supports __getitem__() and __len__(), but is considered a mapping rather than a sequence because the lookups use arbitrary *immutable* keys rather than integers.

The collections.abc.Sequence abstract base class defines a much richer interface that goes beyond just __getitem__() and __len__(), adding count(), index(), __contains__(), and __reversed__(). Types that implement this expanded interface can be registered explicitly using register().

single dispatch A form of *generic function* dispatch where the implementation is chosen based on the type of a single argument.

slice An object usually containing a portion of a *sequence*. A slice is created using the subscript notation, [] with colons between numbers when several are given, such as in variable_name[1:3:5]. The bracket (subscript) notation uses slice objects internally.

special method A method that is called implicitly by Python to execute a certain operation on a type, such as addition. Such methods have names starting and ending with double underscores. Special methods are documented in *Special method names*.

statement A statement is part of a suite (a "block" of code). A statement is either an *expression* or one of several constructs with a keyword, such as *if*, *while* or *for*.

struct sequence A tuple with named elements. Struct sequences expose an interface similar to *named tuple* in that elements can either be accessed either by index or as an attribute. However, they do not have any of the named tuple methods like _make() or _asdict(). Examples of struct sequences include sys.float_info and the return value of os.stat().

text encoding A codec which encodes Unicode strings to bytes.

text file A *file object* able to read and write str objects. Often, a text file actually accesses a byte-oriented datastream and handles the *text encoding* automatically. Examples of text files are files opened in text mode ('r' or 'w'), sys.stdin, sys.stdout, and instances of io.StringIO.

See also:

A *binary file* reads and write bytes objects.

triple-quoted string A string which is bound by three instances of either a quotation mark (") or an apostrophe ('). While they don't provide any functionality not available with single-quoted strings, they are useful for a number of reasons. They allow you to include unescaped single and double quotes within a string and they can span multiple lines without the use of the continuation character, making them especially useful when writing docstrings.

type The type of a Python object determines what kind of object it is; every object has a type. An object's type is accessible as its `__class__` attribute or can be retrieved with `type(obj)`.

universal newlines A manner of interpreting text streams in which all of the following are recognized as ending a line: the Unix end-of-line convention `'\n'`, the Windows convention `'\r\n'`, and the old Macintosh convention `'\r'`. See PEP 278 and PEP 3116, as well as `bytes.splitlines()` for an additional use.

variable annotation A type metadata value associated with a module global variable or a class attribute. Its syntax is explained in section *Annotated assignment statements*. Annotations are stored in the `__annotations__` special attribute of a class or module object and can be accessed using `typing.get_type_hints()`.

Python itself does not assign any particular meaning to variable annotations. They are intended to be interpreted by third-party libraries or type checking tools. See PEP 526, PEP 484 which describe some of their potential uses.

virtual environment A cooperatively isolated runtime environment that allows Python users and applications to install and upgrade Python distribution packages without interfering with the behaviour of other Python applications running on the same system.

See also `venv`.

virtual machine A computer defined entirely in software. Python's virtual machine executes the *bytecode* emitted by the bytecode compiler.

Zen of Python Listing of Python design principles and philosophies that are helpful in understanding and using the language. The listing can be found by typing "`import this`" at the interactive prompt.

ABOUT THESE DOCUMENTS

These documents are generated from reStructuredText sources by Sphinx, a document processor specifically written for the Python documentation.

Development of the documentation and its toolchain is an entirely volunteer effort, just like Python itself. If you want to contribute, please take a look at the reporting-bugs page for information on how to do so. New volunteers are always welcome!

Many thanks go to:

- Fred L. Drake, Jr., the creator of the original Python documentation toolset and writer of much of the content;
- the Docutils project for creating reStructuredText and the Docutils suite;
- Fredrik Lundh for his Alternative Python Reference project from which Sphinx got many good ideas.

B.1 Contributors to the Python Documentation

Many people have contributed to the Python language, the Python standard library, and the Python documentation. See Misc/ACKS in the Python source distribution for a partial list of contributors.

It is only with the input and contributions of the Python community that Python has such wonderful documentation – Thank You!

HISTORY AND LICENSE

C.1 History of the software

Python was created in the early 1990s by Guido van Rossum at Stichting Mathematisch Centrum (CWI, see https://www.cwi.nl/) in the Netherlands as a successor of a language called ABC. Guido remains Python's principal author, although it includes many contributions from others.

In 1995, Guido continued his work on Python at the Corporation for National Research Initiatives (CNRI, see https://www.cnri.reston.va.us/) in Reston, Virginia where he released several versions of the software.

In May 2000, Guido and the Python core development team moved to BeOpen.com to form the BeOpen PythonLabs team. In October of the same year, the PythonLabs team moved to Digital Creations (now Zope Corporation; see http://www.zope.com/). In 2001, the Python Software Foundation (PSF, see https://www.python.org/psf/) was formed, a non-profit organization created specifically to own Python-related Intellectual Property. Zope Corporation is a sponsoring member of the PSF.

All Python releases are Open Source (see https://opensource.org/ for the Open Source Definition). Historically, most, but not all, Python releases have also been GPL-compatible; the table below summarizes the various releases.

Release	Derived from	Year	Owner	GPL compatible?
0.9.0 thru 1.2	n/a	1991-1995	CWI	yes
1.3 thru 1.5.2	1.2	1995-1999	CNRI	yes
1.6	1.5.2	2000	CNRI	no
2.0	1.6	2000	BeOpen.com	no
1.6.1	1.6	2001	CNRI	no
2.1	2.0+1.6.1	2001	PSF	no
2.0.1	2.0+1.6.1	2001	PSF	yes
2.1.1	2.1+2.0.1	2001	PSF	yes
2.1.2	2.1.1	2002	PSF	yes
2.1.3	2.1.2	2002	PSF	yes
2.2 and above	2.1.1	2001-now	PSF	yes

Note: GPL-compatible doesn't mean that we're distributing Python under the GPL. All Python licenses, unlike the GPL, let you distribute a modified version without making your changes open source. The GPL-compatible licenses make it possible to combine Python with other software that is released under the GPL; the others don't.

Thanks to the many outside volunteers who have worked under Guido's direction to make these releases possible.

C.2 Terms and conditions for accessing or otherwise using Python

C.2.1 PSF LICENSE AGREEMENT FOR PYTHON 3.6.4

1. This LICENSE AGREEMENT is between the Python Software Foundation ("PSF"), and the Individual or Organization ("Licensee") accessing and otherwise using Python 3.6.4 software in source or binary form and its associated documentation.

2. Subject to the terms and conditions of this License Agreement, PSF hereby grants Licensee a nonexclusive, royalty-free, world-wide license to reproduce, analyze, test, perform and/or display publicly, prepare derivative works, distribute, and otherwise use Python 3.6.4 alone or in any derivative version, provided, however, that PSF's License Agreement and PSF's notice of copyright, i.e., "Copyright © 2001-2018 Python Software Foundation; All Rights Reserved" are retained in Python 3.6.4 alone or in any derivative version prepared by Licensee.

3. In the event Licensee prepares a derivative work that is based on or incorporates Python 3.6.4 or any part thereof, and wants to make the derivative work available to others as provided herein, then Licensee hereby agrees to include in any such work a brief summary of the changes made to Python 3.6.4.

4. PSF is making Python 3.6.4 available to Licensee on an "AS IS" basis. PSF MAKES NO REPRESENTATIONS OR WARRANTIES, EXPRESS OR IMPLIED. BY WAY OF EXAMPLE, BUT NOT LIMITATION, PSF MAKES NO AND DISCLAIMS ANY REPRESENTATION OR WARRANTY OF MERCHANTABILITY OR FITNESS FOR ANY PARTICULAR PURPOSE OR THAT THE USE OF PYTHON 3.6.4 WILL NOT INFRINGE ANY THIRD PARTY RIGHTS.

5. PSF SHALL NOT BE LIABLE TO LICENSEE OR ANY OTHER USERS OF PYTHON 3.6.4 FOR ANY INCIDENTAL, SPECIAL, OR CONSEQUENTIAL DAMAGES OR LOSS AS A RESULT OF MODIFYING, DISTRIBUTING, OR OTHERWISE USING PYTHON 3.6.4, OR ANY DERIVATIVE THEREOF, EVEN IF ADVISED OF THE POSSIBILITY THEREOF.

6. This License Agreement will automatically terminate upon a material breach of its terms and conditions.

7. Nothing in this License Agreement shall be deemed to create any relationship of agency, partnership, or joint venture between PSF and Licensee. This License Agreement does not grant permission to use PSF trademarks or trade name in a trademark sense to endorse or promote products or services of Licensee, or any third party.

8. By copying, installing or otherwise using Python 3.6.4, Licensee agrees to be bound by the terms and conditions of this License Agreement.

C.2.2 BEOPEN.COM LICENSE AGREEMENT FOR PYTHON 2.0

BEOPEN PYTHON OPEN SOURCE LICENSE AGREEMENT VERSION 1

```
1. This LICENSE AGREEMENT is between BeOpen.com ("BeOpen"), having an office at
   160 Saratoga Avenue, Santa Clara, CA 95051, and the Individual or Organization
   ("Licensee") accessing and otherwise using this software in source or binary
```

form and its associated documentation ("the Software").

2. Subject to the terms and conditions of this BeOpen Python License Agreement,
   BeOpen hereby grants Licensee a non-exclusive, royalty-free, world-wide license
   to reproduce, analyze, test, perform and/or display publicly, prepare derivative
   works, distribute, and otherwise use the Software alone or in any derivative
   version, provided, however, that the BeOpen Python License is retained in the
   Software, alone or in any derivative version prepared by Licensee.

3. BeOpen is making the Software available to Licensee on an "AS IS" basis.
   BEOPEN MAKES NO REPRESENTATIONS OR WARRANTIES, EXPRESS OR IMPLIED. BY WAY OF
   EXAMPLE, BUT NOT LIMITATION, BEOPEN MAKES NO AND DISCLAIMS ANY REPRESENTATION OR
   WARRANTY OF MERCHANTABILITY OR FITNESS FOR ANY PARTICULAR PURPOSE OR THAT THE
   USE OF THE SOFTWARE WILL NOT INFRINGE ANY THIRD PARTY RIGHTS.

4. BEOPEN SHALL NOT BE LIABLE TO LICENSEE OR ANY OTHER USERS OF THE SOFTWARE FOR
   ANY INCIDENTAL, SPECIAL, OR CONSEQUENTIAL DAMAGES OR LOSS AS A RESULT OF USING,
   MODIFYING OR DISTRIBUTING THE SOFTWARE, OR ANY DERIVATIVE THEREOF, EVEN IF
   ADVISED OF THE POSSIBILITY THEREOF.

5. This License Agreement will automatically terminate upon a material breach of
   its terms and conditions.

6. This License Agreement shall be governed by and interpreted in all respects
   by the law of the State of California, excluding conflict of law provisions.
   Nothing in this License Agreement shall be deemed to create any relationship of
   agency, partnership, or joint venture between BeOpen and Licensee. This License
   Agreement does not grant permission to use BeOpen trademarks or trade names in a
   trademark sense to endorse or promote products or services of Licensee, or any
   third party. As an exception, the "BeOpen Python" logos available at
   http://www.pythonlabs.com/logos.html may be used according to the permissions
   granted on that web page.

7. By copying, installing or otherwise using the software, Licensee agrees to be
   bound by the terms and conditions of this License Agreement.

C.2.3 CNRI LICENSE AGREEMENT FOR PYTHON 1.6.1

1. This LICENSE AGREEMENT is between the Corporation for National Research
   Initiatives, having an office at 1895 Preston White Drive, Reston, VA 20191
   ("CNRI"), and the Individual or Organization ("Licensee") accessing and
   otherwise using Python 1.6.1 software in source or binary form and its
   associated documentation.

2. Subject to the terms and conditions of this License Agreement, CNRI hereby
   grants Licensee a nonexclusive, royalty-free, world-wide license to reproduce,
   analyze, test, perform and/or display publicly, prepare derivative works,
   distribute, and otherwise use Python 1.6.1 alone or in any derivative version,
   provided, however, that CNRI's License Agreement and CNRI's notice of copyright,
   i.e., "Copyright © 1995-2001 Corporation for National Research Initiatives; All
   Rights Reserved" are retained in Python 1.6.1 alone or in any derivative version
   prepared by Licensee. Alternately, in lieu of CNRI's License Agreement,
   Licensee may substitute the following text (omitting the quotes): "Python 1.6.1
   is made available subject to the terms and conditions in CNRI's License
   Agreement. This Agreement together with Python 1.6.1 may be located on the
   Internet using the following unique, persistent identifier (known as a handle):

1895.22/1013. This Agreement may also be obtained from a proxy server on the
Internet using the following URL: http://hdl.handle.net/1895.22/1013."

3. In the event Licensee prepares a derivative work that is based on or
   incorporates Python 1.6.1 or any part thereof, and wants to make the derivative
   work available to others as provided herein, then Licensee hereby agrees to
   include in any such work a brief summary of the changes made to Python 1.6.1.

4. CNRI is making Python 1.6.1 available to Licensee on an "AS IS" basis. CNRI
   MAKES NO REPRESENTATIONS OR WARRANTIES, EXPRESS OR IMPLIED. BY WAY OF EXAMPLE,
   BUT NOT LIMITATION, CNRI MAKES NO AND DISCLAIMS ANY REPRESENTATION OR WARRANTY
   OF MERCHANTABILITY OR FITNESS FOR ANY PARTICULAR PURPOSE OR THAT THE USE OF
   PYTHON 1.6.1 WILL NOT INFRINGE ANY THIRD PARTY RIGHTS.

5. CNRI SHALL NOT BE LIABLE TO LICENSEE OR ANY OTHER USERS OF PYTHON 1.6.1 FOR
   ANY INCIDENTAL, SPECIAL, OR CONSEQUENTIAL DAMAGES OR LOSS AS A RESULT OF
   MODIFYING, DISTRIBUTING, OR OTHERWISE USING PYTHON 1.6.1, OR ANY DERIVATIVE
   THEREOF, EVEN IF ADVISED OF THE POSSIBILITY THEREOF.

6. This License Agreement will automatically terminate upon a material breach of
   its terms and conditions.

7. This License Agreement shall be governed by the federal intellectual property
   law of the United States, including without limitation the federal copyright
   law, and, to the extent such U.S. federal law does not apply, by the law of the
   Commonwealth of Virginia, excluding Virginia's conflict of law provisions.
   Notwithstanding the foregoing, with regard to derivative works based on Python
   1.6.1 that incorporate non-separable material that was previously distributed
   under the GNU General Public License (GPL), the law of the Commonwealth of
   Virginia shall govern this License Agreement only as to issues arising under or
   with respect to Paragraphs 4, 5, and 7 of this License Agreement. Nothing in
   this License Agreement shall be deemed to create any relationship of agency,
   partnership, or joint venture between CNRI and Licensee. This License Agreement
   does not grant permission to use CNRI trademarks or trade name in a trademark
   sense to endorse or promote products or services of Licensee, or any third
   party.

8. By clicking on the "ACCEPT" button where indicated, or by copying, installing
   or otherwise using Python 1.6.1, Licensee agrees to be bound by the terms and
   conditions of this License Agreement.

C.2.4 CWI LICENSE AGREEMENT FOR PYTHON 0.9.0 THROUGH 1.2

Copyright © 1991 - 1995, Stichting Mathematisch Centrum Amsterdam, The
Netherlands. All rights reserved.

Permission to use, copy, modify, and distribute this software and its
documentation for any purpose and without fee is hereby granted, provided that
the above copyright notice appear in all copies and that both that copyright
notice and this permission notice appear in supporting documentation, and that
the name of Stichting Mathematisch Centrum or CWI not be used in advertising or
publicity pertaining to distribution of the software without specific, written
prior permission.

STICHTING MATHEMATISCH CENTRUM DISCLAIMS ALL WARRANTIES WITH REGARD TO THIS
SOFTWARE, INCLUDING ALL IMPLIED WARRANTIES OF MERCHANTABILITY AND FITNESS, IN NO

```
EVENT SHALL STICHTING MATHEMATISCH CENTRUM BE LIABLE FOR ANY SPECIAL, INDIRECT
OR CONSEQUENTIAL DAMAGES OR ANY DAMAGES WHATSOEVER RESULTING FROM LOSS OF USE,
DATA OR PROFITS, WHETHER IN AN ACTION OF CONTRACT, NEGLIGENCE OR OTHER TORTIOUS
ACTION, ARISING OUT OF OR IN CONNECTION WITH THE USE OR PERFORMANCE OF THIS
SOFTWARE.
```

C.3 Licenses and Acknowledgements for Incorporated Software

This section is an incomplete, but growing list of licenses and acknowledgements for third-party software incorporated in the Python distribution.

C.3.1 Mersenne Twister

The `_random` module includes code based on a download from http://www.math.sci.hiroshima-u.ac.jp/ ~m-mat/MT/MT2002/emt19937ar.html. The following are the verbatim comments from the original code:

```
A C-program for MT19937, with initialization improved 2002/1/26.
Coded by Takuji Nishimura and Makoto Matsumoto.

Before using, initialize the state by using init_genrand(seed)
or init_by_array(init_key, key_length).

Copyright (C) 1997 - 2002, Makoto Matsumoto and Takuji Nishimura,
All rights reserved.

Redistribution and use in source and binary forms, with or without
modification, are permitted provided that the following conditions
are met:

 1. Redistributions of source code must retain the above copyright
    notice, this list of conditions and the following disclaimer.

 2. Redistributions in binary form must reproduce the above copyright
    notice, this list of conditions and the following disclaimer in the
    documentation and/or other materials provided with the distribution.

 3. The names of its contributors may not be used to endorse or promote
    products derived from this software without specific prior written
    permission.

THIS SOFTWARE IS PROVIDED BY THE COPYRIGHT HOLDERS AND CONTRIBUTORS
"AS IS" AND ANY EXPRESS OR IMPLIED WARRANTIES, INCLUDING, BUT NOT
LIMITED TO, THE IMPLIED WARRANTIES OF MERCHANTABILITY AND FITNESS FOR
A PARTICULAR PURPOSE ARE DISCLAIMED.  IN NO EVENT SHALL THE COPYRIGHT OWNER OR
CONTRIBUTORS BE LIABLE FOR ANY DIRECT, INDIRECT, INCIDENTAL, SPECIAL,
EXEMPLARY, OR CONSEQUENTIAL DAMAGES (INCLUDING, BUT NOT LIMITED TO,
PROCUREMENT OF SUBSTITUTE GOODS OR SERVICES; LOSS OF USE, DATA, OR
PROFITS; OR BUSINESS INTERRUPTION) HOWEVER CAUSED AND ON ANY THEORY OF
LIABILITY, WHETHER IN CONTRACT, STRICT LIABILITY, OR TORT (INCLUDING
NEGLIGENCE OR OTHERWISE) ARISING IN ANY WAY OUT OF THE USE OF THIS
SOFTWARE, EVEN IF ADVISED OF THE POSSIBILITY OF SUCH DAMAGE.


Any feedback is very welcome.
```

```
http://www.math.sci.hiroshima-u.ac.jp/~m-mat/MT/emt.html
email: m-mat @ math.sci.hiroshima-u.ac.jp (remove space)
```

C.3.2 Sockets

The socket module uses the functions, getaddrinfo(), and getnameinfo(), which are coded in separate
source files from the WIDE Project, http://www.wide.ad.jp/.

```
Copyright (C) 1995, 1996, 1997, and 1998 WIDE Project.
All rights reserved.

Redistribution and use in source and binary forms, with or without
modification, are permitted provided that the following conditions
are met:
1. Redistributions of source code must retain the above copyright
   notice, this list of conditions and the following disclaimer.
2. Redistributions in binary form must reproduce the above copyright
   notice, this list of conditions and the following disclaimer in the
   documentation and/or other materials provided with the distribution.
3. Neither the name of the project nor the names of its contributors
   may be used to endorse or promote products derived from this software
   without specific prior written permission.

THIS SOFTWARE IS PROVIDED BY THE PROJECT AND CONTRIBUTORS ``AS IS'' AND
ANY EXPRESS OR IMPLIED WARRANTIES, INCLUDING, BUT NOT LIMITED TO, THE
IMPLIED WARRANTIES OF MERCHANTABILITY AND FITNESS FOR A PARTICULAR PURPOSE
ARE DISCLAIMED.  IN NO EVENT SHALL THE PROJECT OR CONTRIBUTORS BE LIABLE
FOR ANY DIRECT, INDIRECT, INCIDENTAL, SPECIAL, EXEMPLARY, OR CONSEQUENTIAL
DAMAGES (INCLUDING, BUT NOT LIMITED TO, PROCUREMENT OF SUBSTITUTE GOODS
OR SERVICES; LOSS OF USE, DATA, OR PROFITS; OR BUSINESS INTERRUPTION)
HOWEVER CAUSED AND ON ANY THEORY OF LIABILITY, WHETHER IN CONTRACT, STRICT
LIABILITY, OR TORT (INCLUDING NEGLIGENCE OR OTHERWISE) ARISING IN ANY WAY
OUT OF THE USE OF THIS SOFTWARE, EVEN IF ADVISED OF THE POSSIBILITY OF
SUCH DAMAGE.
```

C.3.3 Floating point exception control

The source for the fpectl module includes the following notice:

```
--------------------------------------------------------------------
/                       Copyright (c) 1996.                          \
|           The Regents of the University of California.              |
|                       All rights reserved.                         |
|                                                                    |
|   Permission to use, copy, modify, and distribute this software for |
|   any purpose without fee is hereby granted, provided that this en- |
|   tire notice is included in all copies of any software which is or |
|   includes  a  copy  or  modification  of  this software and in all |
|   copies of the supporting documentation for such software.         |
|                                                                    |
|   This  work was produced at the University of California, Lawrence |
|   Livermore National Laboratory under  contract  no.  W-7405-ENG-48 |
|   between  the  U.S.  Department  of  Energy and The Regents of the |
|   University of California for the operation of UC LLNL.            |
|                                                                    |
```

```
|                           DISCLAIMER                          |
|                                                               |
|    This  software was prepared as an account of work sponsored by an    |
|    agency of the United States Government. Neither the United States    |
|    Government  nor the University of California nor any of their em-     |
|    ployees, makes any warranty, express or implied, or  assumes  any    |
|    liability  or  responsibility  for the accuracy, completeness, or    |
|    usefulness of any information, apparatus,  product,  or  process     |
|    disclosed,   or  represents  that  its  use  would  not  infringe    |
|    privately-owned rights. Reference herein to any specific  commer-    |
|    cial  products,  process,  or  service  by trade name, trademark,    |
|    manufacturer, or otherwise, does not  necessarily  constitute  or    |
|    imply  its  endorsement, recommendation, or favoring by the United   |
|    States Government or the University of California. The views  and    |
|    opinions  of authors expressed herein do not necessarily state or    |
|    reflect those of the United States Government or  the  University     |
|    of  California,  and shall not be used for advertising or product     |
\    endorsement purposes.                                              /
  ---------------------------------------------------------------------
```

C.3.4 Asynchronous socket services

The asynchat and asyncore modules contain the following notice:

```
Copyright 1996 by Sam Rushing

                All Rights Reserved

Permission to use, copy, modify, and distribute this software and
its documentation for any purpose and without fee is hereby
granted, provided that the above copyright notice appear in all
copies and that both that copyright notice and this permission
notice appear in supporting documentation, and that the name of Sam
Rushing not be used in advertising or publicity pertaining to
distribution of the software without specific, written prior
permission.

SAM RUSHING DISCLAIMS ALL WARRANTIES WITH REGARD TO THIS SOFTWARE,
INCLUDING ALL IMPLIED WARRANTIES OF MERCHANTABILITY AND FITNESS, IN
NO EVENT SHALL SAM RUSHING BE LIABLE FOR ANY SPECIAL, INDIRECT OR
CONSEQUENTIAL DAMAGES OR ANY DAMAGES WHATSOEVER RESULTING FROM LOSS
OF USE, DATA OR PROFITS, WHETHER IN AN ACTION OF CONTRACT,
NEGLIGENCE OR OTHER TORTIOUS ACTION, ARISING OUT OF OR IN
CONNECTION WITH THE USE OR PERFORMANCE OF THIS SOFTWARE.
```

C.3.5 Cookie management

The http.cookies module contains the following notice:

```
Copyright 2000 by Timothy O'Malley <timo@alum.mit.edu>

                All Rights Reserved

Permission to use, copy, modify, and distribute this software
and its documentation for any purpose and without fee is hereby
```

```
granted, provided that the above copyright notice appear in all
copies and that both that copyright notice and this permission
notice appear in supporting documentation, and that the name of
Timothy O'Malley  not be used in advertising or publicity
pertaining to distribution of the software without specific, written
prior permission.

Timothy O'Malley DISCLAIMS ALL WARRANTIES WITH REGARD TO THIS
SOFTWARE, INCLUDING ALL IMPLIED WARRANTIES OF MERCHANTABILITY
AND FITNESS, IN NO EVENT SHALL Timothy O'Malley BE LIABLE FOR
ANY SPECIAL, INDIRECT OR CONSEQUENTIAL DAMAGES OR ANY DAMAGES
WHATSOEVER RESULTING FROM LOSS OF USE, DATA OR PROFITS,
WHETHER IN AN ACTION OF CONTRACT, NEGLIGENCE OR OTHER TORTIOUS
ACTION, ARISING OUT OF OR IN CONNECTION WITH THE USE OR
PERFORMANCE OF THIS SOFTWARE.
```

C.3.6 Execution tracing

The `trace` module contains the following notice:

```
portions copyright 2001, Autonomous Zones Industries, Inc., all rights...
err...  reserved and offered to the public under the terms of the
Python 2.2 license.
Author: Zooko O'Whielacronx
http://zooko.com/
mailto:zooko@zooko.com

Copyright 2000, Mojam Media, Inc., all rights reserved.
Author: Skip Montanaro

Copyright 1999, Bioreason, Inc., all rights reserved.
Author: Andrew Dalke

Copyright 1995-1997, Automatrix, Inc., all rights reserved.
Author: Skip Montanaro

Copyright 1991-1995, Stichting Mathematisch Centrum, all rights reserved.


Permission to use, copy, modify, and distribute this Python software and
its associated documentation for any purpose without fee is hereby
granted, provided that the above copyright notice appears in all copies,
and that both that copyright notice and this permission notice appear in
supporting documentation, and that the name of neither Automatrix,
Bioreason or Mojam Media be used in advertising or publicity pertaining to
distribution of the software without specific, written prior permission.
```

C.3.7 UUencode and UUdecode functions

The `uu` module contains the following notice:

```
Copyright 1994 by Lance Ellinghouse
Cathedral City, California Republic, United States of America.
                    All Rights Reserved
Permission to use, copy, modify, and distribute this software and its
```

```
documentation for any purpose and without fee is hereby granted,
provided that the above copyright notice appear in all copies and that
both that copyright notice and this permission notice appear in
supporting documentation, and that the name of Lance Ellinghouse
not be used in advertising or publicity pertaining to distribution
of the software without specific, written prior permission.
LANCE ELLINGHOUSE DISCLAIMS ALL WARRANTIES WITH REGARD TO
THIS SOFTWARE, INCLUDING ALL IMPLIED WARRANTIES OF MERCHANTABILITY AND
FITNESS, IN NO EVENT SHALL LANCE ELLINGHOUSE CENTRUM BE LIABLE
FOR ANY SPECIAL, INDIRECT OR CONSEQUENTIAL DAMAGES OR ANY DAMAGES
WHATSOEVER RESULTING FROM LOSS OF USE, DATA OR PROFITS, WHETHER IN AN
ACTION OF CONTRACT, NEGLIGENCE OR OTHER TORTIOUS ACTION, ARISING OUT
OF OR IN CONNECTION WITH THE USE OR PERFORMANCE OF THIS SOFTWARE.

Modified by Jack Jansen, CWI, July 1995:
- Use binascii module to do the actual line-by-line conversion
  between ascii and binary. This results in a 1000-fold speedup. The C
  version is still 5 times faster, though.
- Arguments more compliant with Python standard
```

C.3.8 XML Remote Procedure Calls

The `xmlrpc.client` module contains the following notice:

```
    The XML-RPC client interface is

Copyright (c) 1999-2002 by Secret Labs AB
Copyright (c) 1999-2002 by Fredrik Lundh

By obtaining, using, and/or copying this software and/or its
associated documentation, you agree that you have read, understood,
and will comply with the following terms and conditions:

Permission to use, copy, modify, and distribute this software and
its associated documentation for any purpose and without fee is
hereby granted, provided that the above copyright notice appears in
all copies, and that both that copyright notice and this permission
notice appear in supporting documentation, and that the name of
Secret Labs AB or the author not be used in advertising or publicity
pertaining to distribution of the software without specific, written
prior permission.

SECRET LABS AB AND THE AUTHOR DISCLAIMS ALL WARRANTIES WITH REGARD
TO THIS SOFTWARE, INCLUDING ALL IMPLIED WARRANTIES OF MERCHANT-
ABILITY AND FITNESS.  IN NO EVENT SHALL SECRET LABS AB OR THE AUTHOR
BE LIABLE FOR ANY SPECIAL, INDIRECT OR CONSEQUENTIAL DAMAGES OR ANY
DAMAGES WHATSOEVER RESULTING FROM LOSS OF USE, DATA OR PROFITS,
WHETHER IN AN ACTION OF CONTRACT, NEGLIGENCE OR OTHER TORTIOUS
ACTION, ARISING OUT OF OR IN CONNECTION WITH THE USE OR PERFORMANCE
OF THIS SOFTWARE.
```

C.3.9 test_epoll

The `test_epoll` module contains the following notice:

```
Copyright (c) 2001-2006 Twisted Matrix Laboratories.

Permission is hereby granted, free of charge, to any person obtaining
a copy of this software and associated documentation files (the
"Software"), to deal in the Software without restriction, including
without limitation the rights to use, copy, modify, merge, publish,
distribute, sublicense, and/or sell copies of the Software, and to
permit persons to whom the Software is furnished to do so, subject to
the following conditions:

The above copyright notice and this permission notice shall be
included in all copies or substantial portions of the Software.

THE SOFTWARE IS PROVIDED "AS IS", WITHOUT WARRANTY OF ANY KIND,
EXPRESS OR IMPLIED, INCLUDING BUT NOT LIMITED TO THE WARRANTIES OF
MERCHANTABILITY, FITNESS FOR A PARTICULAR PURPOSE AND
NONINFRINGEMENT. IN NO EVENT SHALL THE AUTHORS OR COPYRIGHT HOLDERS BE
LIABLE FOR ANY CLAIM, DAMAGES OR OTHER LIABILITY, WHETHER IN AN ACTION
OF CONTRACT, TORT OR OTHERWISE, ARISING FROM, OUT OF OR IN CONNECTION
WITH THE SOFTWARE OR THE USE OR OTHER DEALINGS IN THE SOFTWARE.
```

C.3.10 Select kqueue

The `select` module contains the following notice for the kqueue interface:

```
Copyright (c) 2000 Doug White, 2006 James Knight, 2007 Christian Heimes
All rights reserved.

Redistribution and use in source and binary forms, with or without
modification, are permitted provided that the following conditions
are met:
1. Redistributions of source code must retain the above copyright
   notice, this list of conditions and the following disclaimer.
2. Redistributions in binary form must reproduce the above copyright
   notice, this list of conditions and the following disclaimer in the
   documentation and/or other materials provided with the distribution.

THIS SOFTWARE IS PROVIDED BY THE AUTHOR AND CONTRIBUTORS ``AS IS'' AND
ANY EXPRESS OR IMPLIED WARRANTIES, INCLUDING, BUT NOT LIMITED TO, THE
IMPLIED WARRANTIES OF MERCHANTABILITY AND FITNESS FOR A PARTICULAR PURPOSE
ARE DISCLAIMED.  IN NO EVENT SHALL THE AUTHOR OR CONTRIBUTORS BE LIABLE
FOR ANY DIRECT, INDIRECT, INCIDENTAL, SPECIAL, EXEMPLARY, OR CONSEQUENTIAL
DAMAGES (INCLUDING, BUT NOT LIMITED TO, PROCUREMENT OF SUBSTITUTE GOODS
OR SERVICES; LOSS OF USE, DATA, OR PROFITS; OR BUSINESS INTERRUPTION)
HOWEVER CAUSED AND ON ANY THEORY OF LIABILITY, WHETHER IN CONTRACT, STRICT
LIABILITY, OR TORT (INCLUDING NEGLIGENCE OR OTHERWISE) ARISING IN ANY WAY
OUT OF THE USE OF THIS SOFTWARE, EVEN IF ADVISED OF THE POSSIBILITY OF
SUCH DAMAGE.
```

C.3.11 SipHash24

The file `Python/pyhash.c` contains Marek Majkowski' implementation of Dan Bernstein's SipHash24 algorithm. The contains the following note:

```
<MIT License>
Copyright (c) 2013  Marek Majkowski <marek@popcount.org>

Permission is hereby granted, free of charge, to any person obtaining a copy
of this software and associated documentation files (the "Software"), to deal
in the Software without restriction, including without limitation the rights
to use, copy, modify, merge, publish, distribute, sublicense, and/or sell
copies of the Software, and to permit persons to whom the Software is
furnished to do so, subject to the following conditions:

The above copyright notice and this permission notice shall be included in
all copies or substantial portions of the Software.
</MIT License>

Original location:
   https://github.com/majek/csiphash/

Solution inspired by code from:
   Samuel Neves (supercop/crypto_auth/siphash24/little)
   djb (supercop/crypto_auth/siphash24/little2)
   Jean-Philippe Aumasson (https://131002.net/siphash/siphash24.c)
```

C.3.12 strtod and dtoa

The file `Python/dtoa.c`, which supplies C functions dtoa and strtod for conversion of C doubles to and from strings, is derived from the file of the same name by David M. Gay, currently available from http://www.netlib.org/fp/. The original file, as retrieved on March 16, 2009, contains the following copyright and licensing notice:

```
/****************************************************************
 *
 * The author of this software is David M. Gay.
 *
 * Copyright (c) 1991, 2000, 2001 by Lucent Technologies.
 *
 * Permission to use, copy, modify, and distribute this software for any
 * purpose without fee is hereby granted, provided that this entire notice
 * is included in all copies of any software which is or includes a copy
 * or modification of this software and in all copies of the supporting
 * documentation for such software.
 *
 * THIS SOFTWARE IS BEING PROVIDED "AS IS", WITHOUT ANY EXPRESS OR IMPLIED
 * WARRANTY.  IN PARTICULAR, NEITHER THE AUTHOR NOR LUCENT MAKES ANY
 * REPRESENTATION OR WARRANTY OF ANY KIND CONCERNING THE MERCHANTABILITY
 * OF THIS SOFTWARE OR ITS FITNESS FOR ANY PARTICULAR PURPOSE.
 *
 ****************************************************************/
```

C.3.13 OpenSSL

The modules `hashlib`, `posix`, `ssl`, `crypt` use the OpenSSL library for added performance if made available by the operating system. Additionally, the Windows and Mac OS X installers for Python may include a copy of the OpenSSL libraries, so we include a copy of the OpenSSL license here:

```
LICENSE ISSUES
==============

The OpenSSL toolkit stays under a dual license, i.e. both the conditions of
the OpenSSL License and the original SSLeay license apply to the toolkit.
See below for the actual license texts. Actually both licenses are BSD-style
Open Source licenses. In case of any license issues related to OpenSSL
please contact openssl-core@openssl.org.

OpenSSL License
---------------

  /* ====================================================================
   * Copyright (c) 1998-2008 The OpenSSL Project.  All rights reserved.
   *
   * Redistribution and use in source and binary forms, with or without
   * modification, are permitted provided that the following conditions
   * are met:
   *
   * 1. Redistributions of source code must retain the above copyright
   *    notice, this list of conditions and the following disclaimer.
   *
   * 2. Redistributions in binary form must reproduce the above copyright
   *    notice, this list of conditions and the following disclaimer in
   *    the documentation and/or other materials provided with the
   *    distribution.
   *
   * 3. All advertising materials mentioning features or use of this
   *    software must display the following acknowledgment:
   *    "This product includes software developed by the OpenSSL Project
   *    for use in the OpenSSL Toolkit. (http://www.openssl.org/)"
   *
   * 4. The names "OpenSSL Toolkit" and "OpenSSL Project" must not be used to
   *    endorse or promote products derived from this software without
   *    prior written permission. For written permission, please contact
   *    openssl-core@openssl.org.
   *
   * 5. Products derived from this software may not be called "OpenSSL"
   *    nor may "OpenSSL" appear in their names without prior written
   *    permission of the OpenSSL Project.
   *
   * 6. Redistributions of any form whatsoever must retain the following
   *    acknowledgment:
   *    "This product includes software developed by the OpenSSL Project
   *    for use in the OpenSSL Toolkit (http://www.openssl.org/)"
   *
   * THIS SOFTWARE IS PROVIDED BY THE OpenSSL PROJECT ``AS IS'' AND ANY
   * EXPRESSED OR IMPLIED WARRANTIES, INCLUDING, BUT NOT LIMITED TO, THE
   * IMPLIED WARRANTIES OF MERCHANTABILITY AND FITNESS FOR A PARTICULAR
   * PURPOSE ARE DISCLAIMED.  IN NO EVENT SHALL THE OpenSSL PROJECT OR
   * ITS CONTRIBUTORS BE LIABLE FOR ANY DIRECT, INDIRECT, INCIDENTAL,
   * SPECIAL, EXEMPLARY, OR CONSEQUENTIAL DAMAGES (INCLUDING, BUT
   * NOT LIMITED TO, PROCUREMENT OF SUBSTITUTE GOODS OR SERVICES;
   * LOSS OF USE, DATA, OR PROFITS; OR BUSINESS INTERRUPTION)
   * HOWEVER CAUSED AND ON ANY THEORY OF LIABILITY, WHETHER IN CONTRACT,
   * STRICT LIABILITY, OR TORT (INCLUDING NEGLIGENCE OR OTHERWISE)
   * ARISING IN ANY WAY OUT OF THE USE OF THIS SOFTWARE, EVEN IF ADVISED
   * OF THE POSSIBILITY OF SUCH DAMAGE.
```

```
 *  ====================================================================
 *
 * This product includes cryptographic software written by Eric Young
 * (eay@cryptsoft.com).  This product includes software written by Tim
 * Hudson (tjh@cryptsoft.com).
 *
 */

Original SSLeay License
-----------------------

 /* Copyright (C) 1995-1998 Eric Young (eay@cryptsoft.com)
  * All rights reserved.
  *
  * This package is an SSL implementation written
  * by Eric Young (eay@cryptsoft.com).
  * The implementation was written so as to conform with Netscapes SSL.
  *
  * This library is free for commercial and non-commercial use as long as
  * the following conditions are aheared to.  The following conditions
  * apply to all code found in this distribution, be it the RC4, RSA,
  * lhash, DES, etc., code; not just the SSL code.  The SSL documentation
  * included with this distribution is covered by the same copyright terms
  * except that the holder is Tim Hudson (tjh@cryptsoft.com).
  *
  * Copyright remains Eric Young's, and as such any Copyright notices in
  * the code are not to be removed.
  * If this package is used in a product, Eric Young should be given attribution
  * as the author of the parts of the library used.
  * This can be in the form of a textual message at program startup or
  * in documentation (online or textual) provided with the package.
  *
  * Redistribution and use in source and binary forms, with or without
  * modification, are permitted provided that the following conditions
  * are met:
  * 1. Redistributions of source code must retain the copyright
  *    notice, this list of conditions and the following disclaimer.
  * 2. Redistributions in binary form must reproduce the above copyright
  *    notice, this list of conditions and the following disclaimer in the
  *    documentation and/or other materials provided with the distribution.
  * 3. All advertising materials mentioning features or use of this software
  *    must display the following acknowledgement:
  *    "This product includes cryptographic software written by
  *     Eric Young (eay@cryptsoft.com)"
  *    The word 'cryptographic' can be left out if the rouines from the library
  *    being used are not cryptographic related :-).
  * 4. If you include any Windows specific code (or a derivative thereof) from
  *    the apps directory (application code) you must include an acknowledgement:
  *    "This product includes software written by Tim Hudson (tjh@cryptsoft.com)"
  *
  * THIS SOFTWARE IS PROVIDED BY ERIC YOUNG ``AS IS'' AND
  * ANY EXPRESS OR IMPLIED WARRANTIES, INCLUDING, BUT NOT LIMITED TO, THE
  * IMPLIED WARRANTIES OF MERCHANTABILITY AND FITNESS FOR A PARTICULAR PURPOSE
  * ARE DISCLAIMED.  IN NO EVENT SHALL THE AUTHOR OR CONTRIBUTORS BE LIABLE
  * FOR ANY DIRECT, INDIRECT, INCIDENTAL, SPECIAL, EXEMPLARY, OR CONSEQUENTIAL
  * DAMAGES (INCLUDING, BUT NOT LIMITED TO, PROCUREMENT OF SUBSTITUTE GOODS
  * OR SERVICES; LOSS OF USE, DATA, OR PROFITS; OR BUSINESS INTERRUPTION)
  * HOWEVER CAUSED AND ON ANY THEORY OF LIABILITY, WHETHER IN CONTRACT, STRICT
```

```
* LIABILITY, OR TORT (INCLUDING NEGLIGENCE OR OTHERWISE) ARISING IN ANY WAY
* OUT OF THE USE OF THIS SOFTWARE, EVEN IF ADVISED OF THE POSSIBILITY OF
* SUCH DAMAGE.
*
* The licence and distribution terms for any publically available version or
* derivative of this code cannot be changed.  i.e. this code cannot simply be
* copied and put under another distribution licence
* [including the GNU Public Licence.]
*/
```

C.3.14 expat

The pyexpat extension is built using an included copy of the expat sources unless the build is configured --with-system-expat:

```
Copyright (c) 1998, 1999, 2000 Thai Open Source Software Center Ltd
                    and Clark Cooper

Permission is hereby granted, free of charge, to any person obtaining
a copy of this software and associated documentation files (the
"Software"), to deal in the Software without restriction, including
without limitation the rights to use, copy, modify, merge, publish,
distribute, sublicense, and/or sell copies of the Software, and to
permit persons to whom the Software is furnished to do so, subject to
the following conditions:

The above copyright notice and this permission notice shall be included
in all copies or substantial portions of the Software.

THE SOFTWARE IS PROVIDED "AS IS", WITHOUT WARRANTY OF ANY KIND,
EXPRESS OR IMPLIED, INCLUDING BUT NOT LIMITED TO THE WARRANTIES OF
MERCHANTABILITY, FITNESS FOR A PARTICULAR PURPOSE AND NONINFRINGEMENT.
IN NO EVENT SHALL THE AUTHORS OR COPYRIGHT HOLDERS BE LIABLE FOR ANY
CLAIM, DAMAGES OR OTHER LIABILITY, WHETHER IN AN ACTION OF CONTRACT,
TORT OR OTHERWISE, ARISING FROM, OUT OF OR IN CONNECTION WITH THE
SOFTWARE OR THE USE OR OTHER DEALINGS IN THE SOFTWARE.
```

C.3.15 libffi

The _ctypes extension is built using an included copy of the libffi sources unless the build is configured --with-system-libffi:

```
Copyright (c) 1996-2008  Red Hat, Inc and others.

Permission is hereby granted, free of charge, to any person obtaining
a copy of this software and associated documentation files (the
``Software''), to deal in the Software without restriction, including
without limitation the rights to use, copy, modify, merge, publish,
distribute, sublicense, and/or sell copies of the Software, and to
permit persons to whom the Software is furnished to do so, subject to
the following conditions:

The above copyright notice and this permission notice shall be included
in all copies or substantial portions of the Software.
```

```
THE SOFTWARE IS PROVIDED ``AS IS'', WITHOUT WARRANTY OF ANY KIND,
EXPRESS OR IMPLIED, INCLUDING BUT NOT LIMITED TO THE WARRANTIES OF
MERCHANTABILITY, FITNESS FOR A PARTICULAR PURPOSE AND
NONINFRINGEMENT.  IN NO EVENT SHALL THE AUTHORS OR COPYRIGHT
HOLDERS BE LIABLE FOR ANY CLAIM, DAMAGES OR OTHER LIABILITY,
WHETHER IN AN ACTION OF CONTRACT, TORT OR OTHERWISE, ARISING FROM,
OUT OF OR IN CONNECTION WITH THE SOFTWARE OR THE USE OR OTHER
DEALINGS IN THE SOFTWARE.
```

C.3.16 zlib

The `zlib` extension is built using an included copy of the zlib sources if the zlib version found on the system is too old to be used for the build:

```
Copyright (C) 1995-2011 Jean-loup Gailly and Mark Adler

This software is provided 'as-is', without any express or implied
warranty.  In no event will the authors be held liable for any damages
arising from the use of this software.

Permission is granted to anyone to use this software for any purpose,
including commercial applications, and to alter it and redistribute it
freely, subject to the following restrictions:

1. The origin of this software must not be misrepresented; you must not
   claim that you wrote the original software. If you use this software
   in a product, an acknowledgment in the product documentation would be
   appreciated but is not required.

2. Altered source versions must be plainly marked as such, and must not be
   misrepresented as being the original software.

3. This notice may not be removed or altered from any source distribution.

Jean-loup Gailly        Mark Adler
jloup@gzip.org          madler@alumni.caltech.edu
```

C.3.17 cfuhash

The implementation of the hash table used by the `tracemalloc` is based on the cfuhash project:

```
Copyright (c) 2005 Don Owens
All rights reserved.

This code is released under the BSD license:

Redistribution and use in source and binary forms, with or without
modification, are permitted provided that the following conditions
are met:

  * Redistributions of source code must retain the above copyright
    notice, this list of conditions and the following disclaimer.

  * Redistributions in binary form must reproduce the above
    copyright notice, this list of conditions and the following
```

```
         disclaimer in the documentation and/or other materials provided
         with the distribution.

     *  Neither the name of the author nor the names of its
        contributors may be used to endorse or promote products derived
        from this software without specific prior written permission.

THIS SOFTWARE IS PROVIDED BY THE COPYRIGHT HOLDERS AND CONTRIBUTORS
"AS IS" AND ANY EXPRESS OR IMPLIED WARRANTIES, INCLUDING, BUT NOT
LIMITED TO, THE IMPLIED WARRANTIES OF MERCHANTABILITY AND FITNESS
FOR A PARTICULAR PURPOSE ARE DISCLAIMED. IN NO EVENT SHALL THE
COPYRIGHT OWNER OR CONTRIBUTORS BE LIABLE FOR ANY DIRECT, INDIRECT,
INCIDENTAL, SPECIAL, EXEMPLARY, OR CONSEQUENTIAL DAMAGES
(INCLUDING, BUT NOT LIMITED TO, PROCUREMENT OF SUBSTITUTE GOODS OR
SERVICES; LOSS OF USE, DATA, OR PROFITS; OR BUSINESS INTERRUPTION)
HOWEVER CAUSED AND ON ANY THEORY OF LIABILITY, WHETHER IN CONTRACT,
STRICT LIABILITY, OR TORT (INCLUDING NEGLIGENCE OR OTHERWISE)
ARISING IN ANY WAY OUT OF THE USE OF THIS SOFTWARE, EVEN IF ADVISED
OF THE POSSIBILITY OF SUCH DAMAGE.
```

C.3.18 libmpdec

The `_decimal` module is built using an included copy of the libmpdec library unless the build is configured `--with-system-libmpdec`:

```
Copyright (c) 2008-2016 Stefan Krah. All rights reserved.

Redistribution and use in source and binary forms, with or without
modification, are permitted provided that the following conditions
are met:

1. Redistributions of source code must retain the above copyright
   notice, this list of conditions and the following disclaimer.

2. Redistributions in binary form must reproduce the above copyright
   notice, this list of conditions and the following disclaimer in the
   documentation and/or other materials provided with the distribution.

THIS SOFTWARE IS PROVIDED BY THE AUTHOR AND CONTRIBUTORS "AS IS" AND
ANY EXPRESS OR IMPLIED WARRANTIES, INCLUDING, BUT NOT LIMITED TO, THE
IMPLIED WARRANTIES OF MERCHANTABILITY AND FITNESS FOR A PARTICULAR PURPOSE
ARE DISCLAIMED.  IN NO EVENT SHALL THE AUTHOR OR CONTRIBUTORS BE LIABLE
FOR ANY DIRECT, INDIRECT, INCIDENTAL, SPECIAL, EXEMPLARY, OR CONSEQUENTIAL
DAMAGES (INCLUDING, BUT NOT LIMITED TO, PROCUREMENT OF SUBSTITUTE GOODS
OR SERVICES; LOSS OF USE, DATA, OR PROFITS; OR BUSINESS INTERRUPTION)
HOWEVER CAUSED AND ON ANY THEORY OF LIABILITY, WHETHER IN CONTRACT, STRICT
LIABILITY, OR TORT (INCLUDING NEGLIGENCE OR OTHERWISE) ARISING IN ANY WAY
OUT OF THE USE OF THIS SOFTWARE, EVEN IF ADVISED OF THE POSSIBILITY OF
SUCH DAMAGE.
```

COPYRIGHT

Symbols

*

    in expression lists, 82
    in function calls, 74
    statement, 103

**

    in dictionary displays, 68
    in function calls, 75
    statement, 103

**=

    augmented assignment, 88

*=

    augmented assignment, 88

+=

    augmented assignment, 88

-=

    augmented assignment, 88

..., 113

//=

    augmented assignment, 88

/=

    augmented assignment, 88

: package

    namespace, 52
    portion, 52

=

    assignment statement, 86

%=

    augmented assignment, 88

&=

    augmented assignment, 88

___abs___() (object method), 40
___add___() (object method), 39
___aenter___() (object method), 44
___aexit___() (object method), 44
___aiter___() (object method), 43
___all___ (optional module attribute), 93
___and___() (object method), 39
___anext___() (agen method), 71
___anext___() (object method), 43
___annotations___ (class attribute), 23
___annotations___ (function attribute), 21

___annotations___ (module attribute), 23
___await___() (object method), 42
___bases___ (class attribute), 23
___bool___() (object method), 29, 37
___bytes___() (object method), 28
___cached___, 58
___call___() (object method), 37, 75
___cause___ (exception attribute), 91
___class___ (instance attribute), 24
___class___ (method cell), 35
___class___ (module attribute), 30
___classcell___ (class namespace entry), 35
___closure___ (function attribute), 21
___code___ (function attribute), 21
___complex___() (object method), 40
___contains___() (object method), 38
___context___ (exception attribute), 91
___debug___, 89
___defaults___ (function attribute), 21
___del___() (object method), 27
___delattr___() (object method), 30
___delete___() (object method), 31
___delitem___() (object method), 38
___dict___ (class attribute), 23
___dict___ (function attribute), 21
___dict___ (instance attribute), 24
___dict___ (module attribute), 23
___dir___() (object method), 30
___divmod___() (object method), 39
___doc___ (class attribute), 23
___doc___ (function attribute), 21
___doc___ (method attribute), 21
___doc___ (module attribute), 23
___enter___() (object method), 41
___eq___() (object method), 28
___exit___() (object method), 41
___file___, 58
___file___ (module attribute), 23
___float___() (object method), 40
___floordiv___() (object method), 39
___format___() (object method), 28
___func___ (method attribute), 21

built-in function, 40
number, 19
object, 19
complex literal, 13
complex number, 115
compound
    statement, 97
comprehensions
    list, 67
Conditional
    expression, 81
conditional
    expression, 82
constant, 9
constructor
    class, 26
container, 18, 23
context manager, 40, 115
contiguous, 115
continue
    statement, 92, 98, 100
conversion
    arithmetic, 65
    string, 28, 85
coroutine, 42, 69, 115
    function, 22
coroutine function, 115
CPython, 115

D

dangling
    else, 97
data, 17
    type, 18
    type, immutable, 66
datum, 67
dbm.gnu
    module, 20
dbm.ndbm
    module, 20
debugging
    assertions, 89
decimal literal, 13
decorator, 115
DEDENT token, 7, 97
def
    statement, 102
default
    parameter value, 103
definition
    class, 90, 104
    function, 90, 102
del
    statement, 27, 89

deletion
    attribute, 90
    target, 89
    target list, 89
delimiters, 15
descriptor, 115
destructor, 27, 86
dictionary, 116
    display, 67
    object, 20, 23, 29, 67, 72, 87
dictionary view, 116
display
    dictionary, 67
    list, 67
    set, 67
    tuple, 66
division, 77
divmod
    built-in function, 39
docstring, 104, 116
documentation string, 24
duck-typing, 116

E

EAFP, 116
elif
    keyword, 98
Ellipsis
    object, 18
else
    dangling, 97
    keyword, 92, 98, 100
empty
    list, 67
    tuple, 19, 66
encoding declarations (source file), 5
environment, 48
environment variable
    PYTHONHASHSEED, 29
error handling, 49
errors, 49
escape sequence, 10
eval
    built-in function, 95, 108
evaluation
    order, 83
exc_info (in module sys), 25
except
    keyword, 99
exception, 49, 91
    AssertionError, 89
    AttributeError, 72
    chaining, 91
    GeneratorExit, 70, 72

namespace, 21
    statement, 90, 95
global interpreter lock, 117
grammar, 4
grouping, 7

H

handle an exception, 49
handler
    exception, 25
hash
    built-in function, 29
hash character, 5
hashable, 68, 118
hexadecimal literal, 13
hierarchy
    type, 18
hooks
    import, 54
    meta, 54
    path, 54

I

id
    built-in function, 17
identifier, 8, 65
identity
    test, 81
identity of an object, 17
IDLE, 118
if
    statement, 98
imaginary literal, 13
immutable, 118
    data type, 66
    object, 19, 66, 68
immutable object, 17
immutable sequence
    object, 19
immutable types
    subclassing, 26
import
    hooks, 54
    statement, 23, 92
import hooks, 54
import machinery, 51
import path, 118
importer, 118
ImportError
    exception, 93
importing, 118
in
    keyword, 98
    operator, 81

inclusive
    or, 78
INDENT token, 7
indentation, 7
index operation, 19
indices() (slice method), 25
inheritance, 104
input, 108
instance
    call, 37, 75
    class, 23
    object, 23, 75
int
    built-in function, 40
integer, 19
    object, 18
    representation, 19
integer literal, 13
interactive, 118
interactive mode, 107
internal type, 24
interpolated string literal, 12
interpreted, 118
interpreter, 107
interpreter shutdown, 118
inversion, 76
invocation, 20
io
    module, 24
is
    operator, 81
is not
    operator, 81
item
    sequence, 72
    string, 73
item selection, 19
iterable, 118
    unpacking, 82
iterator, 119

J

Java
    language, 19

K

key, 67
key function, 119
key/datum pair, 67
keyword, 9
    async, 105
    await, 105
    elif, 98
    else, 92, 98, 100

except, 99
finally, 90, 92, 99, 100
from, 92, 93
in, 98
yield, 68
keyword argument, 119

L

lambda, 119
    expression, 82, 103
    form, 82
language
    C, 18, 19, 22, 78
    Java, 19
last_traceback (in module sys), 25
LBYL, 119
leading whitespace, 7
len
    built-in function, 19, 20, 37
lexical analysis, 5
lexical definitions, 4
line continuation, 6
line joining, 5, 6
line structure, 5
list, 119
    assignment, target, 86
    comprehensions, 67
    deletion target, 89
    display, 67
    empty, 67
    expression, 82, 85
    object, 20, 67, 72, 73, 87
    target, 86, 98
list comprehension, 119
literal, 9, 66
loader, 53, 119
logical line, 5
loop
    over mutable sequence, 99
    statement, 92, 98
loop control
    target, 92

M

makefile() (socket method), 24
mangling
    name, 66
mapping, 119
    object, 20, 24, 72, 87
matrix multiplication, 76
membership
    test, 81
meta
    hooks, 54

meta hooks, 54
meta path finder, 120
metaclass, 34, 120
metaclass hint, 34
method, 120
    built-in, 22
    call, 75
    object, 21, 22, 75
    user-defined, 21
method resolution order, 120
minus, 76
module, 120
    __main__, 48, 107
    array, 20
    builtins, 107
    dbm.gnu, 20
    dbm.ndbm, 20
    extension, 18
    importing, 92
    io, 24
    namespace, 23
    object, 23, 72
    sys, 100, 107
module spec, 53, 120
modulo, 77
MRO, 120
multiplication, 76
mutable, 120
    object, 20, 86, 87
mutable object, 17
mutable sequence
    loop over, 99
    object, 20

N

name, 8, 47, 65
    binding, 47, 86, 92, 93, 102, 104
    binding, global, 95
    class, 104
    function, 102
    mangling, 66
    rebinding, 86
    unbinding, 90
named tuple, 120
NameError
    exception, 65
NameError (built-in exception), 48
names
    private, 66
namespace, 47, 120
    : package, 52
    global, 21
    module, 23
namespace package, 120

writing
    values, 85

X

xor
    bitwise, 78

Y

yield
    examples, 70
    expression, 68
    keyword, 68
    statement, 90

Z

Zen of Python, 124
ZeroDivisionError
    exception, 77